EDIROTIAL

Welcome to the latest edition of Eastern Heroes, a special edition dedicated to the movie "Accident Man: Hitman's Holiday"! We are beyond excited to delve into this incredible film, which boasts an incredible cast including the talented Scott Adkins and the visionary directors George and Harry Kirby.

"Accident Man: Hitman's Holiday" is a movie that delivers an exhilarating and action-packed experience, filled with Hong Kong-style combat and a perfect blend of humour and charm. I was privileged to sit down with Scott Adkins and some of the cast members, as well as the Kirby brothers, to gain exclusive insights into the making of this exceptional film.

With Scott Adkins leading the way as the ultimate action hero, "Accident Man: Hitman's Holiday" captivated audiences around the world with its stunning visuals, top-notch performances, and masterful direction. This film stands out as a true gem in the action movie genre, and we are thrilled to explore what makes it so special.

Join us as we dive deep into the making of "Accident Man: Hitman's Holiday" and uncover the secrets behind this cinematic masterpiece. So sit back, relax, and get ready to experience one of the most exhilarating and exciting action movies of 2022!

ACCIDENT MAN
HITMAN'S HOLIDAY

Review By Rick Baker

Accident Man: Hitman's Holiday (2022)
*Directed by: Harry & George Kirby
Cast: Scott Adkins, Ray Stevenson, Perry Benson, Sarah Chang, Javad Ramezani, George Fouracres, Flaminia Cinque, Beau Fowler, Faisal Mohammed.*

Accident Man 2: Hitman's Holiday is an elevated, action-packed sequel that delivers on all fronts. Director George Kirby, alongside his co-director and brother Harry Kirby, manages to maintain the same British tone of the original while ramping up the action sequences to a whole new level. The movie features an impressive cast of co-stars, with Scott Adkins leading the way as Mike Fallon, the Accident Man. Some of the standout additions to the sequel include Sarah Chang, who plays Su Lin, a descendant of Wong Fei Hung. Chang's fight scene against Adkins in his apartment are a delight of action and comedy, showcasing the distinct Hong Kong flair of the choreography style, with plenty of prop breakage thrown in for good measure.

The fight scenes in the movie are well-executed, with Adkins and his hand-picked team of fighters delivering an adrenaline-pumping experience that leaves audiences on the edge of their seats.

The supporting cast also delivers impressive performances, with Ray Stevenson reprising his role as Adkins' mentor and Perry Benson returning as assassin Finnicky Fred. Peter Lee Thomas, Faisal Mohammed and George Fouracres all add an extra layer of depth to the movie, with an exceptional performance from Beau Fowler as "Poco" the Clown.

The setting of Malta provides a stunning backdrop for the movie, with Adkins and Stu Smalls script is well-crafted, with Adkins taking on a hit job targeting the son of a fearsome mafia heiress, who hires him to keep her son safe. The arrival of five of the world's best assassins looking to make the hit adds an extra layer of tension, with Adkins relying on his fists and feet to fight his way out of trouble.

Overall, Accident Man 2: Hitman's Holiday is a must-see for fans of Hong Kong comedy action peppered with British humour. With its well-executed fight scenes, impressive cast, and solid storyline, the movie delivers on all fronts. Adkins and his team of co-stars and choreographers have done an excellent job of bringing the sequel to life, and it's definitely was one of the big action movies for 2022.

HARRY KIRBY

Harry Kirby is a British director, composer, and co-producer known for his work in the film industry. He has a master's degree in music composition from the University of Bristol and has utilized his musical talent in several of his productions.

Kirby made his directorial debut with "Howl" in 2013, followed by the psychological thriller "Ghostboy" in 2015. His most notable work to date is the award-winning British psychological thriller "Twenty Twenty-Four" in 2016, for which he not only directed but also composed the musical score and co-produced the film.

His latest feature, "Accident Man 2: Hitman's Holiday," continues his trend for action and thought-provoking films. With a strong background in music composition and a passion for storytelling, Harry Kirby is a talented and innovative filmmaker who is making a mark in the industry.

GEORGE KIRBY

George Kirby is a talented and experienced stuntman and actor in the entertainment industry. With a passion for performing and a dedication to his craft, he has become a sought-after performer in Hollywood.

Kirby has worked on some of the biggest productions in recent years, including "The Batman," "Justice League," and "Zack Snyder's Justice League." He has also served as a stunt double for some of the biggest names in the business, including Benedict Cumberbatch in "Doctor Strange" and Matt Smith in "Morbius."

His work as a fight coordinator in the Sony Pictures production "Venom: Let There Be Carnage" showcases his versatility and skills as a performer. Additionally, he served as a stunt double for Ewan McGregor in "Christopher Robin."

Kirby's latest project, "Accident Man: Hitman's Holiday," demonstrates his ability to bring excitement and energy to a production. With his talent and experience, George Kirby is a valuable asset to any film production and is destined for continued success in the entertainment industry.

INTERVIEW WITH THE KIRBY BROTHERS

By Rick Baker

From Script to Screen: Harry and George Kirby Discuss Their First Directorial Effort with 'Accident Man 2'

RB: Great to meet you both! Let me kick the interview off by asking you Harry, could you tell us a bit about your background? What experiences and skills have you developed throughout your career?

HK: Certainly! George and I have slightly different backgrounds, but we both shared a passion for film growing up. I started my career in TV, but in order to break into the film industry, we both began creating short films and posting them on YouTube in the hopes of gaining attention.

RB: Absolutely, it's amazing how technology has given rise to so many opportunities for aspiring creative people there was nothing like this in my day.

HK: Yes, YouTube was a great platform for us. Prior to that, we had made a few short films, but we knew that if we wanted to gain more attention, we needed to step up our game. Both George and I are big anime fans, particularly of Dragon-ball Z, so we decided to create a short film inspired by that series. The Dragon-Ball Z short film was a massive hit, garnering millions of views and providing the attention we were looking for. Following that success, we focused on creating action-packed shorts and fan films, such as "Batman" and "The X-Men," where we could showcase exciting fight scenes. George had become a stuntman by that time, which allowed us to draw in other stunt performers and improve the production quality without breaking the bank.

RB: A bit like £100 movies (smiles)

HK: Our budget was quite limited back then, and as I continued to work as a producer for a TV channel - specifically a Poker Channel - our work there had nothing to do with our little production company. However, following the success of our YouTube shorts, we decided to create a proof of concept for a feature film we wanted to produce. By this point, we had made so many shorts that we knew our next goal was to create a feature film.

Our proof of concept was for an action zombie movie, and we were very keen to have Scott appear in it. We believed that attaching his name would help us secure the necessary budget. Fortunately, George had connections with Scott, so we sent him the script. However, he did not want to play the character we had offered him. Despite that, he was impressed by what we had done, so he invited us to direct Accident Man 2, which he was about to start making.

RB: So in this industry you do need an element of good luck to get you on your way

HK: I agree that luck can play a significant role in one's success, but I also believe that it's possible to make your own luck to some extent. By working hard, putting in the effort, and taking calculated risks, you can create opportunities for yourself that may not have been possible otherwise. Ultimately, success is often a combination of hard work, talent, and being in the right place at the right time, which some may attribute to luck.

RB: Persistence always pays of in the end I believe.

HK: Being persistent is the key, as we learned first-hand. Off the back of the "DragonBall Z" shorts we created, we were offered the opportunity to produce a live-action DragonBall Z series with a $4 million budget. However, the owner of the property, Toei Animation, stepped in and prevented the project from moving forward.

Persistence is definitely important in this industry, as is having the necessary skills to back up your ideas. George, for example, has a background in stunts, which has been incredibly valuable in our productions.
RB: yes George tell us a bit about yourself.
GK: Yes, I have been working as a stuntman for over ten years now. I started by joining the British Stunt Register a decade ago, and since then, I've been fortunate enough to work on some big movies.

RB: my impression of people that work in that profession is that it can be quite "clicky" and people seem keeping within the same groups making it a bit hard for any newcomers.

GK: In some cases, the stunt coordinator will choose their own team of stunt performers. If the team works well together and has a good working relationship, they may be hired to work on future productions together. However, the process is not quite the same in the United States. In the US, for instance, there are branded teams like 7-Eleven that are formed and hired as a unit

RB: Who do you work with as a team?

GK: I used to work a lot with a stunt coordinator called Mark Mottram, and I worked alongside Paul Herbert on "Game of Thrones."

RB: So, some pretty big names then!

HK: Yes, I mean that the British Stunt Register will get most of the good jobs out there. They are considered the best in the world, and this has enabled me to work on movies like "Star Wars". I was fortunate enough to double for Benedict Cumberbatch on "Doctor Strange", which is where I actually met Scott. He was one of the characters in the movie, and we had a brief fight scene in which he threw me down some stairs. I have been incredibly lucky.

RB: What made you get into stunts; it's not everybody chosen career is it?

HK: Well, actually, a friend of our dad, a

guy named Jamie Edgell, who was a James Bond double for Pierce Brosnan, used to visit us and tell stories. I think he pretty much planted the seed in my mind that this was what I wanted to do, and that set me on my path. As a kid, I was already doing gymnastics and horse riding, gaining many of the skills that would be needed to become a stunt performer, so I was halfway there. However, I didn't start my training until I was 21. Before that, I did some live TV work, and I actually worked with Harry for a while. But I realized that I wanted to pursue my childhood dream of becoming a stuntman, so I started my training and got on the stunt register.

RB: so going back to you Harry what where your movie influences growing up?

HK: There are lots of different movies that I enjoy, but I am definitely a big fan of Spielberg. I particularly loved "Jurassic Park" and "Jaws". However, I would say that "Jurassic Park" was the movie that influenced me to want to make movies. I was around 11 years old at the time, and I remember coming out of the cinema feeling completely blown away. Seeing my mom and dad also excited about the film confirmed to me that this was what I wanted to do

RB: I remember when Jonathan Ross saw this and he said to me at the time "I swear they were real dinosaurs in that movie. Prior to that I was a Ray Harryhausen fan with all the stop motion and still am, but that movie was just on another level.

HK: I agree! After that, other seminal films like "The Matrix" would have been important to me. I have always been drawn to films with action that have a distinct genre, like sci-fi. I also enjoy action films that have a stylish feel and a good rhythm. I really liked the action in "Hot Fuzz"; the film had a great vibe, especially when the action scenes kicked in. These are my main influences. However, it was actually my brother George who watched more of the traditional Hong Kong action movies. I enjoyed them too, but it was George who was more into them.

RB: So what was your movie influence George?

GK: I was a huge fan of Jackie Chan, particularly films like "Rumble in the Bronx," "Wheels on Meal," and "Operation Condor." Jackie Chan was a massive inspiration to me, to the point where if I went to the local video shop and saw a kung fu movie, I would rent it regardless of the title or who starred in it. I just wanted to watch kung Fu movies! (Laughs) I also started watching Jet Li movies, such as "Hero" and "Fearless." I loved "Crouching Tiger Hidden Dragon," which took Hong Kong movies to a new level of polish, and "House of Flying Daggers," which was a beautifully shot epic fantasy film.

RB: Did you also watch the comedy action of Steven Chow for example "Shaolin Soccer" and "Kung Fu Hustle"?

GK: Yes, loved "Kung Fu Hustle" but I must admit I have not seen "Shaolin Soccer" but one I must watch.

RB: So lets us talk about Accident man Hitmans Holiday I mean I loved the film and I hear you shot those well-choreographed fight sequences in only two days which was incredible.

HK: (laughs) It took two days to film each fight, but many people mistakenly believe that it took two days for the entire movie. Scott, our producer, was fantastic as he urged us to allot at least two days for each fight. Although filming was tight, we managed to push ourselves to our limits. The fights were intense, so we had to go, go, and go!

RB: I had to say you were very ginormous with your fight scenes for the individual actors because often than not a person's time can be under 30 seconds and there out, were as in Accident man 2 each fight was in itself a showcase piece that would have been great for any actor to take away and out on their CV. And what impressed me was to do a British comedy Martial art's film I feel that there are very few people that could carry that off in this country and I thought what you did was a fantastic job.

HK: Thank you very much. It was

definitely a balancing act, and I believe that Scott's English background and exceptional skill, combined with Andy Long's Hong Kong style and a British team, made for a great combination. With Stewart writing the script, it worked out well for us

RB: I have to say, with the British humour and references to "The Pink Panther" with Peter Sellers and Kato, as well as the Hong Kong-style action, I could tell that a great deal of attention had been paid to those fight scenes. Each fight was unique, unlike in some movies where the action is choreographed like fighting by numbers. In my humble opinion, you did a fantastic job!

GK: "With Andy on board, we were able to incorporate the Hong Kong style into the movie. We aimed to give each fight scene its own unique tone and flavour. Particularly in Sarah's scenes, we wanted to keep the mood light and entertaining while showcasing her Wu-Shu skills. On the other hand, Andy's fight was more straightforward and focused on martial arts."

RB: You could see the Jackie Chan references, and the fight with Faisal Mohammed, in particular, was a great scene, despite the challenges you had faced with the rain. All the fight scenes had an abundance of energy and complexity, given the limited time we had to work with.

HK: A lot of it had to do with the previews. We had planned out every fight scene beforehand and shot a rough version, which we could show to the first assistant director on set. This allowed everyone to know what the next shot would entail and enabled Scott and the performers to move seamlessly from one scene to the next. By going from shot to shot, we were able to move through the sequences much quicker. If we had to do any on-the-spot choreography, which we did a little bit, it would have slowed us down and hindered our ability to complete the film

RB: I know that Beau, who played 'Poco the Clown,' had to come in at the last minute, but I thought he brought a lot to his character in addition to his fighting skills. His acting for the part was excellent and added depth to his role.

HK: He was fantastic! Even though he arrived at the last minute, he didn't show up empty-handed and ask, 'Okay, I got nothing. What do you want me to do?' Instead, he showed up with a fully-formed character in his head and shared his vision for how he saw the character on screen. We loved his ideas and gave him the green light. We were fortunate to have him, as our previous actor had to withdraw due to contracting COVID-19 and was immediately placed in isolation at the hotel. But everything worked out well in the end, as Beau delivered everything we could have hoped for

RB: I did love some of the scenes you set up for example Fred when he is creating some of his ideas like the suit how it played out later in the movie, often these could be throwaway scenes but these were well executed and well set up for a later moment in the movie.

GK: Once again, that was something we learned through experience – setting up the scene and then playing it out later. For instance, in the 'Poco' scene, where he could not feel any pain, we were able to show how the accident kills worked by putting him through the wringer. It was great to see the weapons being used on 'Poco,' who could withstand the blows due to his inability to feel pain. This added more to the scene and the story, creating chaos and making it a really fun fight to execute.

RB: Also the annoying kid played very well by George Fouracre was also a good add to the movie I mean I really wanted to see him killed by the end of the movie.
HK: Although Scott is meant to be the hero, there are typically villains as well, so the audience will inevitably want them defeated by the end. As for me, since I like the actor George so much, his character "Dante" was tolerable, despite being a villain. This is because he is a really nice guy off-screen, and I thought his pleasant persona off-screen bled into his on-screen character. However, of course, we knew that the audience would prefer to see him defeated in the end

RB: also Perry brought a lot of good humour to the movie with his cheeky cockney banter

HK: Indeed, Perry is one of the funniest and sweetest guys, and this quality made him effortlessly funny on screen. His mere appearance would make you smile, and he knows how to play his character so well. Additionally, he is quite recognizable to the British audience. George, also enjoyed working with him.

GK: Yes, it was our intention to make Perry's character very likable to the audience. We wanted the audience to feel sorry for him when he gets kidnapped and for "Mike Fallon" to rescue him. This is because they had formed a nice relationship that was somewhat of a bro-mance. Our aim was to make Perry's character as lovable as possible

RB: I believe you managed to make all the characters' parts interesting in the film. Despite the abundance of events in the movie, in my opinion, none of the characters felt unnecessary or like padding. As newcomers directing a feature film, you both did a great job, and I'm not exaggerating. I think you have a bright future ahead of you. Hopefully, your phone will start ringing off the hook, and work offers will come in thick and fast I mean you could be directing the next "John Wick" style movie.

HK: George and I have often discussed that "John Wick" would be our ideal project. We imagine having a decent budget, not necessarily a mega-budget, but enough to allow us to execute some exciting ideas

RB: I had a conversation with Gareth Evans regarding "The Raid", and I mentioned that the violence was great, but it was also quite enjoyable. Putting that aside, we both know that not only did the actors have to be skilled in fighting, but there also had to be a solid script in place to keep the audience engaged from one fight scene to the next so who is going to bring the next level of action to the screen.

HK: it is going to be the Kirby Brothers (smiling)
RB: that's great I can say I interviewed them as they were just starting their journey and I hope as you become rich and famous that I have followed you on your journey and continued to cover you in my magazine.

HK: That would be great and we are glad that you have taken time out to talk to us in your magazine as we know it's well read around the world and thank you for taking the time out to talk to us.

RB: it was a pleasure and look forward to hearing about your next project thank you guys

HK/GK: No thank you Ricky and we look forward to reading the magazine when it comes out.

SARAH CHANG
AN OVERVIEW
By Rick Baker

Sarah Chang is an American actress, producer, stunt coordinator and martial artist who has made a name for herself in the film industry. Her background in Wushu, a Chinese martial art, has allowed her to bring a level of authenticity and skill to her roles that is unmatched by many of her peers.

Growing up in McLean, Virginia, Chang was introduced to Wushu at the age of seven by her father, a fan of Chinese Wu Xia movies. Under the guidance of her first coach, Zhang Guifeng, a teammate of Jet Li on the Beijing Wushu Team, Chang went on to become a US national Wushu champion, a five-time member of the US Wushu Team, and ranked #5 in the world.

Chang's martial arts background served as a bridge into a career in film and television. She first worked in video production, doing stunt choreography for a music video in Taiwan. She then joined Jimmy Hung's action team, working on popular TV series in Taiwan such as My Crossing Hero and Moon River.

After moving to Beijing to study acting at the Central Academy of Drama, Chang landed her first feature film lead role in the multiple award-winning Blood Hunters: Rise of the Hybrids. She has since starred in several other feature films such as Excellent Doctor from Hejian, Barbi: D' Wonder Beki, and The Trigonal: Fight for Justice. Chang also took the leading role in the psycho-horror film Circle of Bones (2020).

In addition to her feature film roles, Chang has also acted in leading roles in award-winning short films such as The Teacher (2018) and We Are War (2018). She has also founded a stunt wire rigging team in Manila called the SACHANG Action Design Team, providing wire rigging stunts for major blockbusters in the Philippines.

Most recently, Chang starred in the film Accident Man Hitman's Holiday and gave a performance that deserves recognition and praise. Her background in martial arts and her dedication to her craft make her a standout in the industry. Chang continues to push the boundaries and is an inspiration to many aspiring actors and martial artists alike.

Page 11 Accident Man: Hitman's Holiday

INTERVIEW WITH SARAH CHANG

By Rick Baker

RB: Sarah before re we dive into our interview, could you please provide our readers with a brief background about yourself? Thank you

SC: Certainly. I've been practicing Wu Shu since the age of 5 and competed on the Wu Shu team for a decade. Afterward, I transitioned to a career in sales and marketing in Asia

RB: May I interject quickly? Typically, when I mention my guest's martial arts background, I often discover that they became actors or stunt performers through a serendipitous encounter or by chance. With that said, did you aspire to become an actress, or how did your career in the film industry begin?

SC: It wasn't until many years later that a friend of mine asked for my help in a music video featuring five girls with an action director. I had a blast helping out, and this led to an introduction to Jimmy Hung, who happens to be Sammo Hung's son. He asked me to join his team, and that's how my career in the film industry began.

RB: So at this time was you still doing your normal day job?

SC: Well, it's actually a funny story. Just before being invited to that shoot, I had decided to quit my job. It was perfect timing because I was getting ready to compete in Wu Shu again here in Taiwan.

RB: Who were your influences when entering the film industry? Donnie Yen and Jet Li, who are also trained in Wu Shu, are well-known in the industry. Were you a fan of their films, and did you watch many Hong Kong films when you were growing up?

SC: Yes, definitely. Hong Kong Cinema had a big influence on me, especially because my Wu Shu friends and I would get together to watch films such as "Once Upon a Time in China" and "Fong Sai Yuk." It was great when "Crouching Tiger Hidden Dragon" was released in America because I thought, 'Wow, now people will get to see these films in the mainstream.' It was an exciting time

R**B: Yes, I had been promoting Hong Kong films since the 80,s it was at the time a pretty much an underground scene, we had brought over both Donnie Yen and Jet Li to try to establish them more to a western audience in the 90's and video releases where getting better, especially with some of the labels I consulted for like "Made In Hong Kong" and Hong Kong Legends" but it was not until "Crouching Tiger Hidden Dragon" got a theatrical release and at the same time it was the Birth of DVD here in the UK so some of these classic films Like Bruce lee, and Jackie Chan were getting released on this new format and elevating martial art films to a new level which influenced a new generation. Did you start Wu shu because you thought it looked like something you would like, or was it due to the movies you had watched when you were younger that attracted you to this style.**

SC: Well, my dad really likes Wu Shu movies, so he (smiling) encouraged his two little daughters to learn it. He also thought it would be good for self-defence. So, partly because of my father and partly because of the movies, I got into it. We used to attend Sunday school to learn Chinese, and there was a coach who happened to be Jet Li's teammate giving classes there. We decided to sign up, and it turned out that we were quite good. He took us into his school, and we started training Wu Shu all the time.

RB: I must say that you are exceptionally good. I've seen many people try to conquer this style, and it's not the easiest, but some are more natural than others and to my eye, you seem to be very much a natural.

SC: Well, at the end of the day, I am so thankful to my dad for kind of forcing me to take up Wu Shu. Doing all that practice and stretching became my true foundation. Starting in my youth really helped because if I had started later in life, I don't think I could have achieved the level of skills I have achieved through all my hard work when I was younger. As I got better, it really developed my passion for Wu Shu because, in the beginning, it felt more like a chore getting through the lessons.

RB: I started practicing martial arts in my early teens with Karate, which

was quite a rigid style. I saw some people teaching Wu Shu and thought it looked great, but at that time, I wasn't flexible enough to become competent, so I stuck to Karate Did you learn weapons as well during your training?

SC: Yes, my early training was just the basics, but then I moved on to the 'Broad Sword' and the 'Straight Sword,' and then the 'Spear.' That was when I truly found my passion and my calling.

RB: Recently, I saw a video of two highly skilled Wu Shu girls doing a demonstration at breakneck speed with spears. They were missing each other by millimetres, but it was so engaging and beautiful to watch.

SC: I Know, I personally have not done the one with the spear poking at my head, but in China some of the athletes there are insane. It looks like there flying and their precision and how well they can handle their body they're totally amazing.

RB: I think to reach that level of skill; they must be training from when they are in nappies (laughs) because the level they reach is like Gold medal Olympic stage, quite incredible. Are you still practising now being a mother and pursuing a film career?

SC: Yes, I am still training, but I have eased up on competition mode as I cannot train at that level anymore. It takes up too much time because everything has to be just perfect

RB: Yes, and being a mom, you have to refocus your priorities. Can I go back to a previous question? You mentioned working on a music video with five girls and being introduced to Timmy Hung. What happened next for you?

SC: Well, I was actually lucky. I got offered the opportunity to double for someone in a straight sword Wu Shu set, which, to be honest, doesn't happen very often in Taiwan. The action director at the time also knew Wu Shu, but he had not performed Wu Shu in a long time, at least in the past five years. So, he said to me, 'Well, this just fell into my lap, and you just fell into my lap.' This led me to be doing stunt double work at that time.

RB: So was your work stunt doubling now doing work in Tiawan?

SC: Yes. for Taiwan Movies and TV series.

RB: TV can be very good work in Taiwan, Hong Kong, and China, I mean they can run for 100 episodes plus so I think its good work if you get the gig. So this allows you to hone your skills and good opportunities to network so what happened next for you?

SC: I discovered that I really liked being in front of the camera, so I decided to take up acting classes. I moved over to Beijing and took whatever opportunities I could get.

RB It's very important if you want to move into action movies that, no matter how good your on-screen fighting is, you must take up acting.

Otherwise, you will only be cast for roles as thugs or the third fighter from the left or background action. So, if you are taking your movie career seriously, you have to invest in yourself, as it's a very competitive industry. The better you can act, the more chance you have of getting more screen time with lines.

SC: That is true. If you are not going to improve your acting skills, then you will end up being just an extra. Since I started taking acting classes, my last stunt double role was for "Wolf Warrior 2," where I was both stunt doubling for Celina Jade and acting in the movie.

RB: So was your first big screen role playing Siu Ling in Accident Man 2?

SC: Yes, in a production of this size, I also did a couple of lead roles in some international Filipino movies

RB: Was those roles that you did in the Philippians more drama based?

SC: Mostly action, but films like "Circle of Bones" had more drama with some action.

RB: With various streaming platforms available, movies can now reach a larger audience. Moreover, you can create a showreel and upload it to YouTube for greater recognition. I had a conversation about this issue with Harry and George Kirby the other night, and they appeared out of nowhere. I like to think that I have my finger on the pulse when it comes to new and upcoming talent. During my interview with Scott, I mentioned that his relationship with you reminded me of "The Pink Panther" movies, with you being like his "Kato." The comedy brought a distinctly British flavour to the screen, and I commented that the casting of Sui Ling was an excellent choice. She demonstrated impressive acting and fighting skills. Scott responded with a lot of praise for you, so our opening conversation was all about you. When you were given that part, how did you approach it?

SC: The first script for my character depicted her as a soft and gentle person, with a possible shift towards romance. There was also a switch in her personality where she could become extremely angry and then revert to her gentle nature. When I read the script, I was okay with it until I came across the part where this kind and sweet girl suddenly beats up Scott Adkins. I thought to myself, "What? This is crazy!" Later, Scott called me and suggested changing the character to be more like the lady in "Kung Fu Hustle." I was immediately interested and agreed to the new approach.

RB: Yes, that's exactly how I saw her on the screen - a younger and more attractive version of Yuen Qiu, who played the Landlady in "Kung Fu Hustle." You know, with the big rollers in her hair and a cigarette hanging from her lips (laughs). One of the things that stood out to me in the movie was how generous Scott was with the entire cast. He allowed them to have great set pieces, giving them the opportunity to showcase their skills on their CVs when applying for future roles. There were no throwaway fight scenes in the movie; all of them were well put together and presented in one-on-one scenarios throughout the film.

SC: You're absolutely right, and I am incredibly grateful for the opportunity to have been part of the movie. I'm even more thankful for the changes Scott made to my character, allowing her to shine through the film. I'm so grateful to Scott and the Kirby Brothers for giving me the chance to portray Sui Ling so well on screen. It was an excellent showcase for my abilities, and they pushed me to do my best. I'm also thankful that they saw something special in my acting and fighting skills,

RB: I mean this showcased your acting, fighting and comedy. I often think to make it in this industry you need that little extra that X-factor to shine out when given the chance.

SC: It was truly a whirlwind time, and it was all thanks to the whole team being there. With two directors, Scott, and Andy Long, it made everything possible.

RB: And it was also a big break for most of the other cast getting to showcase their talents in this movie that would get to be seen by a worldwide audience.

SC: Absolutely, it was a fantastic team to work with. We were all martial artists, which created a great working environment. Everyone was helpful, humble, and hardworking. Even when I was yelling at Scott during the opening scenes, we did a few takes, and Scott encouraged me to just go for it. (Smiles)

RB: I heard that they asked you to scream obscenities in your own language, and apparently, they did not bother to subtitle those outbursts. They still are not sure what you were screaming. Would you care to enlighten me?

SC: That is so funny I remember after the ADR I thought they were going to subtitle it but they did not do it and they left it in.

RB: So they decided to not subtitle it and let your facial expression deliver the words (laughing) and let your anger come flying out.

SC: (Laughing), it's actually quite rude, you know. I don't speak Cantonese, but I have a friend who does. I asked them to tell me the worst words I could use, and the funny thing is, they asked me if I was sure because there are some that are about your mother, and then there are some that are about your mother's genitals. So, I told them I only wanted to hear the ones about the mother, and they said "I will f*ck you in your lungs." Please excuse my language.

RB: let me jump in right there because I asked the Kirby Brothers what does that actually mean and they laughed and said "we don't know" bit let just leave it in. But it was the last word that I would have expected to here at the end of that line.

SC: That is exactly correct when translated. It literally means 'in your lungs!' So, I decided to translate it and see how it would sound

RB: I tell you what I like, I love to go to the screenings and you can gauge a movie from the audiences reaction which was very good at the London screening. Have you managed to see this with an audience?

SC: I actually screened it here in Taipei, but for some reason, my mom wanted to invite one of my aunties and all her friends, who are in their 60s and 70s, to see it. I tried to warn them about my outburst, but I didn't do enough to prepare them. I should have mentioned that the movie is based on a comic book, so it should be viewed in a similar way as a comic book. Instead, I just told them it was a very, very, very violent film, so they should be prepared.

RB: You should have just said

remember its just acting!

SC: well a few of them got the jokes but with the others I think they were totally shocked (laughing)

RB: Also it is very British Humour in the movie so they might have struggled with that as well.

SC: I had a second screening with just my friends, both in the Philippines and Taiwan, and it went really well. Everyone was laughing throughout the entire film. At least my friends loved it

RB : I must admit that I did find the character that George played I did find really annoying. You did want to see him dead at the end and he seems like a really nice guy but if he wanted to achieve hatred from the audience, he did his job very well (laughs)

SC: I just bowed and said I don't know how you prepared for some of the scenes but you did a great job rather you than me.

RB: So as we speak is Accident man now available in your country to stream as it's now available here in the UK.

SC: Yes it went out yesterday here in Tiawan, and its early days but I think It's doing very well

RB: Well Scott does have a big fan base worldwide so I think it will do very well worldwide, and I think since covid people have got more accustomed to watching new releases at home and I think this has created bigger viewing figures for mid-range action movies especially with the price it is to go to the cinema here in London.

SC: yes here in Tiawan it is on YouTube as well.

RB: Talking of YouTube, do you have your own YouTube channel which a lot of today's artists seem to have'

SC: Yes, I do have a YouTube channel where I share family content, including a show called 'The Kung Fu Mamma' show. I am also a producer, and we have a production space where we create small-scale commercials for family products, as well as record our YouTube channels and podcasts. We are planning to do a reboot, and I am hoping that my first guest will be Scott Adkins

RB: SO you interview people from all over and on any subject.

SC: Yes I have done 71 episodes so far and right now it's just for YouTube also when I had my baby I started to interview many people like sleep experts and nutrition experts and early childhood development to help me with advice as a new mum.

RB: So all sounds good, so let me ask you what's up next for Sarah in 2023.

SC: Currently, my focus is to get my name out there and find a reputable international agent after watching the movie.

RB: I believe you have a very promising future ahead of you, and I am certain that we will be seeing more of you in the future. I hope to have the opportunity to catch up with you in a later interview and follow your career, especially after your outstanding performance in "Accidents man 2". Thank you for taking the time to chat with me, and I am excited to see what your next project will be. I look forward to giving you a call to get the latest updates. Thank you, Sarah, it was a pleasure chatting with you

SC: Thank you Ricky, I look forward to reading this in the magazine take care.

CIRCLE of BONES
"The Devil works in mysterious ways"

From multiple award-winning writer/director Vincent Soberano comes a supernatural thriller based on his unpublished book, "Yawa" - a tale of local superstitions and modern-day urban legends of the Visayas region. Set in the picturesque island of Panglao, Bohol, the story is told by a lone survivor of a mysterious cult suspected of mass murders and child sacrifices.

US Distribution: Vertical Entertainment
US Theatrical Release in 10 Major Cities
Cable/Satellite and Digital Release to 100 million homes

Written and Directed by: Vincent Soberano
Genre: Supernatural Thriller
Running time: 80 minutes
Starring: Sarah Chang, Marela Torre, Jana Victoria, Ian Ignacio, Epy Quizon with Filipino film icon Joel Torre and Osric Chau from hit series Supernatural

Logline: A former FBI Agent is questioned regarding a series of murders links to a mysterious demonic cult she had investigated — an unsolved case that left her traumatized, burned, and disfigured.

Synopsis: When Filipino police investigate a lone survivor from a series of bizarre and macabre cult murder-sacrifices that has left a trail of bloody, dismembered bodies and bones, they find a former American FBI agent living in seclusion - disfigured, traumatized and mentally unstable. Her accounts of supernatural events, demonic possessions, ancient prophecies and child sacrifices only sound too incredulous, where lines are blurred, bordering between truth, deception or delusion.

Copyright©2020 by IGP Entertainment Inc. All rights reserved.

5 FINGERS OF DISCS

By Johnny Burnett

Greetings once more Dear Friends, and welcome to this special Scott Adkins powered 5 Fingers of Discs! This issue naturally, our focus is firmly fixed on searching out some lesser known Blu-ray releases of some of Scott's movies, this it turned out, was a bit tricky! Sadly, most of the releases of Scott's movies available here in his native UK, are a bit, well lacking, usually bare bones, which seems a massive shame, when Scott himself has such an amazing Youtube channel and has interviewed lots of his collaborators from his movies, any of these episodes would make for a great on-disc extra for any UK boutique label that may revisit any of his work in the future (fingers crossed)
But for present day, we have to look to our German friends, who have been doing our Boy proud of late with some really, really nice editions of some of Scott's finest.
So with the mind to 'save you going round the Wrekin' I bring you the best of his best…

I'm assuming that most of you reading this S.A special will be familiar with his movies themselves, so i'm mostly just going to focus on the actual physical media releases of the films rather than synopsis etc.

1) **Avengement**
   **Region B Bluray/ DVD Mediabook (several different cover options),
   A Futurepack Bluray (like a Steelbook)
   and a standalone 4k!
   Nameless (Germany)**

Absolutely one of my favorite Scott Adkin's movies, and arguably one of the best new British movies in donkey's years. I had way higher hopes for this great little UK Action / Revenge/ Basher movie getting a decent outing on Physical Media in the UK, sadly it's a pretty lackluster outing here at home, but take a look at the incredible treatment the movie has been given by nameless media in Germany, with an absolute wealth of choices in packaging and format. There are 7 different Media books, a Future pack steebook style case, a 4K edition and for the Uber dedicated collector, a pretty amazing looking Collector's Edition which adds an insanely cool Shotgun Wielding Adkins Bust as well as lots more on disc extras including a commentary track by Scott himself along with exclusive bonus footage housed in a dual language media book (English and German)
all bundled together with a T-Shirt!

Why there is nothing like this back home for Avengement is a total mystery.

2) Ninja / Ninja 2 Double Pack
   Region B
   German Import

Less of a fancy release packaging wise, but just nice to have both of the two excellent Adkins Ninja movies together in one set, the standalone blueRays for the two movies can be a little hard to track down in the UK still. This German double is easily available on Amazon Germany and is usually pretty well priced.
Both the two movies directed by Isaac Florentine are solid martial arts flicks.
No English subtitles on this release, which may be a little tricky in the few places where Japanese is spoken but English Audio tracks are on there for both movies.
To the best of my knowledge, this double pack was briefly available in the UK too, but seems to be out of print.

3) Debt Collector Ltd Ed Mediabooks
   Retro Gold 63
   Blu-ray / DVD

The German's certainly do love their Mediabooks don't they? And thanks to Google translate, you can too! Both the Debt Collector movies got their own nice Blu-Ray/ DVD Mediabooks from Retro Gold 63, not a label I know, so I can't speak to the quality of the discs overall, but the media books themselves look nice and they are quite fairly priced.
Don't let the German language element of these great style of releases put you off, Google translate gets better and better with every upgrade and works pretty well on a phone when you scan each page of text, if you can't be arsed with that nonsense, the pictures are always nice too. And it's the nicest packaging you'll see for the two Debt Collector movies so far, can't speak to the quality of the transfers or discs themselves as this is not a label I know, but they're out there for anyone curious!

4) Undisputed II, III & IV
   Various Worldwide
   Blu-ray

The character Scott plays in the second - forth installments of the undisputed film series, the Russian Prison fighter Yuri Boyka has become a firm fan favorite and remains arguably, the part he's most associated with. Sadly though, physical media releases of the undisputed movies has been a bit of a mixed bag so far.
There is a French box set that groups them all together, but most of the discs released anywhere worldwide are almost entirely bare bones on blu-ray.
The US Region1 DVD of Part 2 did include an Audio commentary by director Isaac Florentine, actors Michael Jai White and Scott Adkins but this seems not to have been ported over onto Bluray, and the two subsequent movies only offer short 10min behind the scenes featurettes. That all being said though, there are a few nice packaging options out there, including this nice Steelbook for Part4… if Steelbooks are your bag, baby.
But it's another series crying out for a 88 Films or 101 Films Black Label boxset here in the UK, with a chance to get the original actors and filmmakers back for interviews and commentaries!

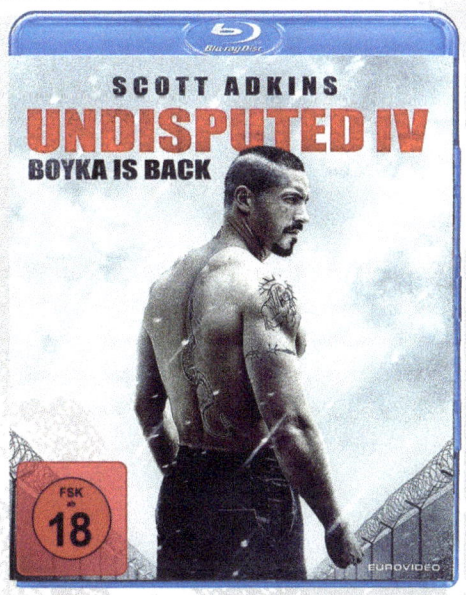

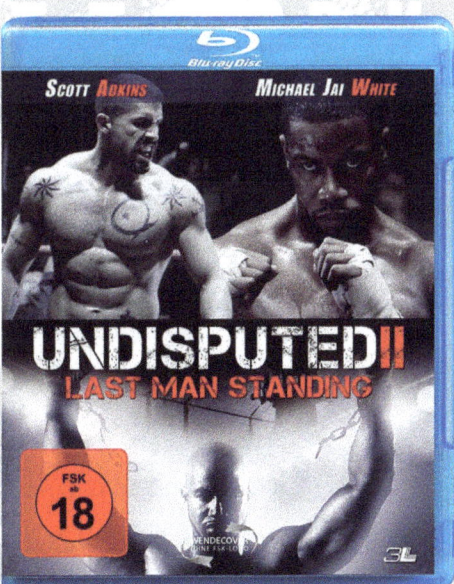

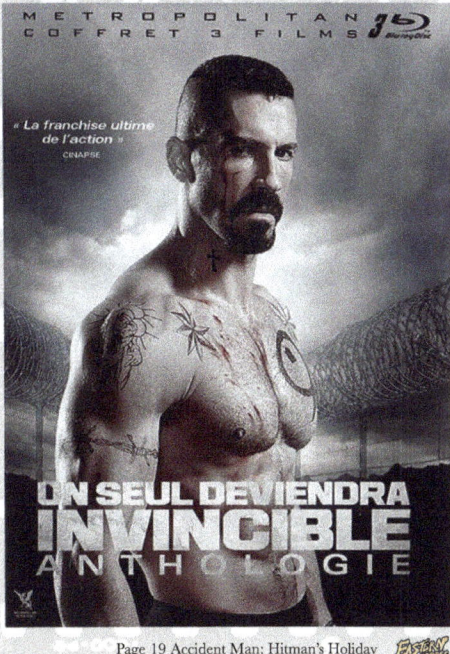

5) Scott Adkins Triple Action Collection (Close Range / Pay Day / Savage Dog)
   Koch Films
   Region B

Last up in this whistle stop tour is a quite nice triple pack, grouping together three more movies Adkins has made with Jesse Johnson and Isaac Florentine:
Close Range, Pay Day and Savage Dog are three pretty solid action features, solidly crafted.
Extras wise, there are short making Of's Soundtracks and Songs and some deleted scenes.

Those are the main releases of Scott's out there in versions that caught my eye for now, hopefully in time we'll see one of the UK labels giving some of Adkins' movies a proper fully booted special edition, they absolutely deserve it!

Triple Threat and Accident Man especially I would have thought both absolutely deserve great special editions, especially given Triple Threat's stellar cast, Iko Uwais, Tiger Chen, and Tony Jaa on hero duties and Michael Jai White and of course, Scott Adkins relishing playing the villains. There are bare bones releases of both pretty widely available.

And whilst that's yer lot as far as our Cover Star's movies go, there are a few other Blu-ray releases I've been really excited about lately that I would be remiss if I didn't include here…..

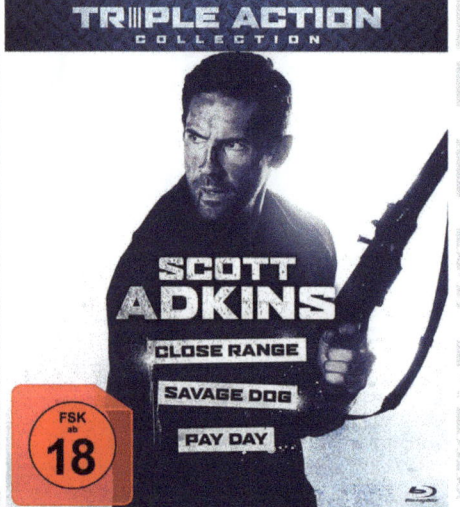

CHAMELEON FILMS

Since the last time I was able to put one of my sections together I've fallen head over heels in love with new Aussie Boutique Blu-ray label Chameleon Films and picked up their first three releases, two slices of pure Johnnie To Magic and one utterly charming Japanese Sci-fi/comedy mashup.. All three arrived beautifully presented in Criterion Style - Scanavo cases with meaty, well written and thoughtful booklets alongside a great showing of on discs extras.

The label is going to be firmly focused on showcasing contemporary Asian cinema. And they've started off very strong indeed!

6) Breaking News - Spine #1
   Chameleon Films
   Region B
   Blu-ray

From the first wave of three releases, this is hands down my favourite title..
Johnnie To's excellent Crime Thriller 'Breaking News' A film that feels weirdly far, far more relevant in todays society than it may have to the audiences when it originally released and examines the Police's attempt to fight a PR war against a gang of thieves who out manuevere the cops in the first act, leaving them looking weak and incapable. The police response is to start a targeted Media campaign to paint themselves in a better, more effective light. Whilst we still have a stack of action sequences, shoot outs, chases and hostage situations here (including one jaw dropping continuous 9 min opening shot) it's all set against a backdrop of media perception and manipulation. The power of the 'narrative' in journalism.
It's shot in a far more documentary and grounded fashion than many of To's other movies, but it's done with such incredible technical precision that it impresses just as much as the more refined and stylised cinematography on display in Exiled the other Johnnie To feature released by Chameleon in this first collection.
On disc extras are impressive too, we get a limited ed collector booklet with essays by Hayley Salon and Mike Walsh a brand new audio commentary by the mighty Frank Djeng
"A Propaganda Duel" - a newly extended video essay on Breaking News (6 mins) and a host of Archival Extras: Melbourne

International Film Festival 2004 Q&A with Johnnie To (19 mins), Two newly unearthed interviews from Cannes 2004 with Johnnie To (12 mins) and Kelly Chen & Nick Cheung* (8 mins), Behind the scenes (3 mins), Deleted scene [Mandarin only] (2 mins), Photo gallery and Theatrical trailer..

7) Summer Timemachine Blues - #2
   Chameleon Films
   Region B
   Blu-ray

Spine #2 from the label introduces a great little low budget Japanese Time Travel comedy Summer Timemachine Blues (from the same writer behind the also fantastic time paradox movie - Beyond The Infinite two Minutes) This charming

little comedy set around a Science club at High school being visited by a student from the Future is deceptively intricate and really well conceived and executed, a great palate cleanser after the visceral intensity of Breaking News! A whimsical and really breezy little movie with lots of tips of the hat to other seminal time travel movies, and a lot of laughs from the excellent performances from the young cast.

Extras wise we again get a Limited first-pressing collector's booklet featuring a new essay by film writer Hayley Scanlon an Original audio commentary by director Katsuyuki Motohiro & writer Makoto Ueda with newly translated English subtitle, New interview with writer Makoto Ueda (21 mins) and a teaser and theatrical trailer.

8) Exiled- #3
Chameleon Films
Region B
Blu-ray

Rounding out the first wave of titles was Johnnie To's Exiled, a much more stylised and as a result, more familiar slice of HK Crime/ Action starring Anthony Wong, one of Johnnie To's most celebrated Gangster movies, a perfectly realised slice of male bonding, heroic bloodshed driven, ultra cool HK cinema.Essential!

Writing in the Limited first-pressing collector's booklet comes this time from by film historian Stephen Teo & Dylan Cheung, We get not one, but TWO brand new audio commentaries by Hong Kong cinema expert Frank Djeng,

"The Weight of Honour" - a new video essay on Exiled (7 mins),
New interview with co-composer Dave Klotz (20 mins),
Newly translated and improved optional English subtitles and the Archival Extras:
Exiled Dreams - The Cult Career of Josie Ho (14 mins), Making of Exiled (12 mins), Behind the scenes (6 mins), Photo gallery, HK trailers x2, US trailer

It's a really solid start of genuinely intriguing titles to kick things off from Chameleon and
the label have been incredibly customer focused since their launch, responded to feedback regarding slipcases for their releases with a short survey campaign on Social
media resulting in them admirably retrospectively producing O-Ring slipcases for all three
of the movies currently released and a committment to include them in all future releases.

I know some folks couldn't care less about the printed extras, but I've long been a fan of
nice design and nice packaging so really do appreciate a label going that extra mile to make sure their customers are getting what they want!

In March Chameleon Films return in style once more to Mr Johnnie To and will put out his sublime HK Crime classics Election 1 & 2 as a double pack,

I'll be covering this release too just as soon as I can get my hands on it!

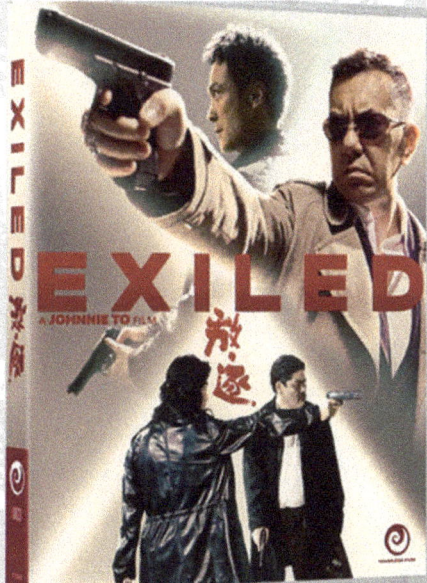

VINEGAR SYNDROME

Over in the USA, Vinegar Syndrome have ben continuing their recent foray into HK cinema (Last year they put out Righting Wrongs and The Iceman Cometh) with some really intriguing choices, since my last article, the label have released two Ringo Lam films, wildly varied from each other in in tone and genre…

9) Burning Paradise
Vinegar Syndrome
Region A
Blu-ray

First released was Burning Paradise, Ringo Lam's Martial Arts spectacular, produced by Tsui Hark and telling another tale in the saga of Fong Sai Yuk set amid the backdrop of the persecution of the Monks from the Shaolin Temple. After fleeing the Manchu forces, Fong Sai Yuk is imprisoned at the

Red Lotus temple where the film takes a definite side step into Indiana Jones and the Temple of Doom territory, with traps galore and some pretty great practical effects. I last saw the film via Made in Hong Kong VHS tape so watching this restoration was like seeing a while new movie! It looks absolutely spectacular and the extras provided were all very solid..
Newly scanned & restored in 2K from its 35mm original camera negative
with a brand new Commentary track with film historian & author Samm Deighan, "A Rare Confidant" (16 min) - a brand new interview with actor Wong Kam Kong, interview with Producer Tsui Hark (5 min), Video essay by filmmaker Chris O'Neill (20 min),
Original theatrical trailer, 12-page booklet with essay by martial arts film historian and author Grady Hendrix and Inside sleeve artwork and slipcase with artwork by Tony Stella,
The release is locked to US Region A Bluray, but Eureka recently revealed that they'll be releasing the movie in the UK on Region B later in 2023. Likely with unique extras.

10) Undeclared War
  Vinegar Syndrome
  Region Free
  Blu-ray

Undeclared War is a bit of an oddity overall, but an entertaining one. released after Burning Paradise by VS, but made before it, in 1990 and showcasing Danny Lee and Rosamund Kwan alongside an international cast including Vernon Wells of Mad Max 2 / Commando / Weird Science fame (here getting to play a master of disguise/ terrorist), Olivia Hussey and Peter Lapis.
VS have been stepping up with solid extras for these releases (their reputation for their cult, horror and exploitation cinema releases is incredibly good) and this release was no exception. It's presented newly scanned & restored in 2K from its 35mm original camera negative in its original Cantonese language soundtrack with newly translated English subtitles, along with a Mandarin language dub track
There is a Brand new commentary track with film historian and author Samm Deighan
"The Business of Revolution" - a brand new interview with actor Vernon Wells
"Undeclared Score" - a brand new

interview with composer Noel Quinlan
Reversible sleeve artwork by Tony Stella

For movie reviews, upcoming Blu-ray release information and unboxing videos and to also be able to chat with other Kung Fu and Martial Arts Blu-ray collectors,

take a minute to jump on over and find me on Youtube, where I post regular updates and new videos every few days.

Written by Johnny 'The Fanatical Dragon' Burnett
www.youtube.com/thefanaticaldragon

Character reviews by Simon Pritchard

Big Ray. Mike's maniacal father figure and mentor from the first film.

Role:
After the first film, Mike and Fred do not want Big Ray to know about the venture in Malta. With Fred informing Big Mike that he's met Mike again and inadvertently giving away their location, when the contract for Dante comes through "Two birds with one stone".
The story progresses and is friendship more important than 9 million Euros?
Ray Stephenson – The actor
Ray is an Irish actor that started his acting career in English television in 1993 and later moved into films in 1998. Ray's filmography has great mix between prime time UK shows and Hollywood films. These include:

- Band of Gold (1995)
- Peak Practice (1997)
- Holby City (2000)
- Waking the Dead (2004)
- King Arthur (2004)
- Punisher: War Zone (2008)
- The Book of Eli (2010)
- Thor (2011)
- Dexter (2012)
- Thor: Dark World (2013)
- Star Wars Rebels (2016 – 2017)
- Thor: Ragnarok (2017)
- Star Wars: The Clone Wars (2020)
- Das Boot (2022)

DANTE ZUUZER

Dante is Mrs. Zuuzer's spoilt brat of a child that is kidnapped.
Role
George Foreacres. Who provides an excellent performance as (purposely), the most irritating character in a long time. Even his mother would shot him! Dante is the target of the assassins and Mike must protect him to ensure he gets back to his mother, and to save his friend.
George Fouracres – The actor
George is a comedian and actor that started his career as a Shakespearean actor. George has starred in:

- Drunk History (2016 -2017)
- Pls Like (2018)
- Spitting Image (2020)
- Don't Hug Me I'm Scared (2022)
- Friday Night Comedy from BBC Radio 4 (2022)

YENDI THE VAMPIRE

An assassin from Ghana who enjoys consuming blood.

Role:
Yendi is one of the assassins out to kill Dante. Yendi drinks victims blood and tell their blood types. He challenges Mike using an axe and machete.

Faisal Mohammed – The actor

Faisal is a British former Kick Boxing World Champion and an undefeated pro Cruiserweight boxer. From his popularity and success as as a martial artist, Faisal moved into films and television, such as:

• The Legend of Tarzan (2016)
• Krypton (2018-2019)
• Are We Dead Yet? (2019)
• Hannah (2020)
• Pennyworth (2020-2021)
• Mia and the Dragon Princess (2022)

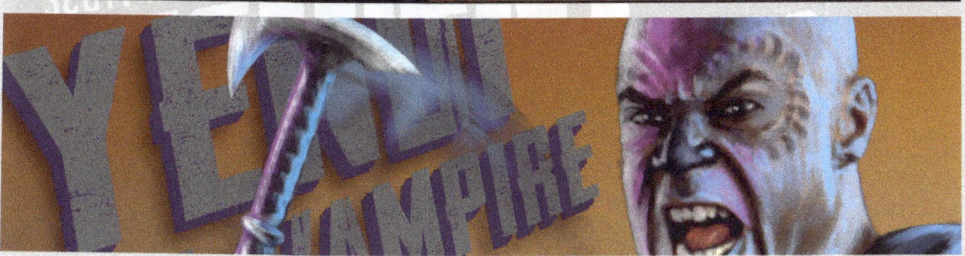

FINERKY FRED

Character overview
Mike is (Scott Atkins) friend from the first film, who specialises in unorthodox weapons.

Role:
After a Fred goes searching for the 'love of his life' he found on the internet, he has coincidental meeting with Mike in Malta. Fred is reintroduced with a flame thrower up his sleeve, burning a doorman with what is presumably napalm. The other two doormen go to attack Fred and Mike intervenes. Fred and Mike rekindle their friendship and go back into business together. After their success in Malta, a contract goes out for Dante Zuuzer, the son of the Mrs. Zuuzer (Flaminia Cinque) local gangster and 'The Don'. Whilst they decline the contract, Fred is kidnapped by Mrs Zuuzer and Mike must protect Dante to get Fred back.

Perry Benson – The actor
Perry started his acting career in 1978 and was an extra in Grange Hill. Perry's television and Movie career went quickly from there. Perry has starred in some of the most classic and cult films to have come out of the UK. These include:

- Scum (1979)
- Quadrophenia (1979)
- Blackadder (1983)
- The Young Ones (1984)
- Sid and Nancy (1986)
- Hi De Hi (1987)
- You Rang, M'Lord? (1988 to 1993)
- Misfits (2009)
- Doctor Who (2010)
- Benidorm (2014 to 2015)
- This is England (2006)
- Sick of it (2018)

SILAS SAN FRANCISCO'S STRANGLER

An assassin who prefers to strangle his victims to death.

Plot

Silas is also one of the assassins out to kill Dante. The good looking 'Brad Pitt' lookalike confronts Mike and holds a gun to him. Poco The Killer Clown (Beau Fowler) enters and during the carnage, Wong Siu-Ling (Sarah Chang) enters and takes on Silas. Will the Siu-Ling be able to become a killer?

Peter Lee Thomas – The actor

Martial Artist and persona trainer to the Stars such as Halle Berry. Peter started as stunt performer in 2007 and has been the stunt coordinator up until 2021. This included the 2013 MTV Movie Awards ceremony. Peter has starred in:

- The Last Sentinel (2007)
- Night of the Templar (2012)
- Game Therapy (2015)
- Timid Tales (2016)
- Doomsday Device (2017)
- Hollow Point (2019)
- Acceleration (2019)

SCOTT ADKINS POSTER GALLERY

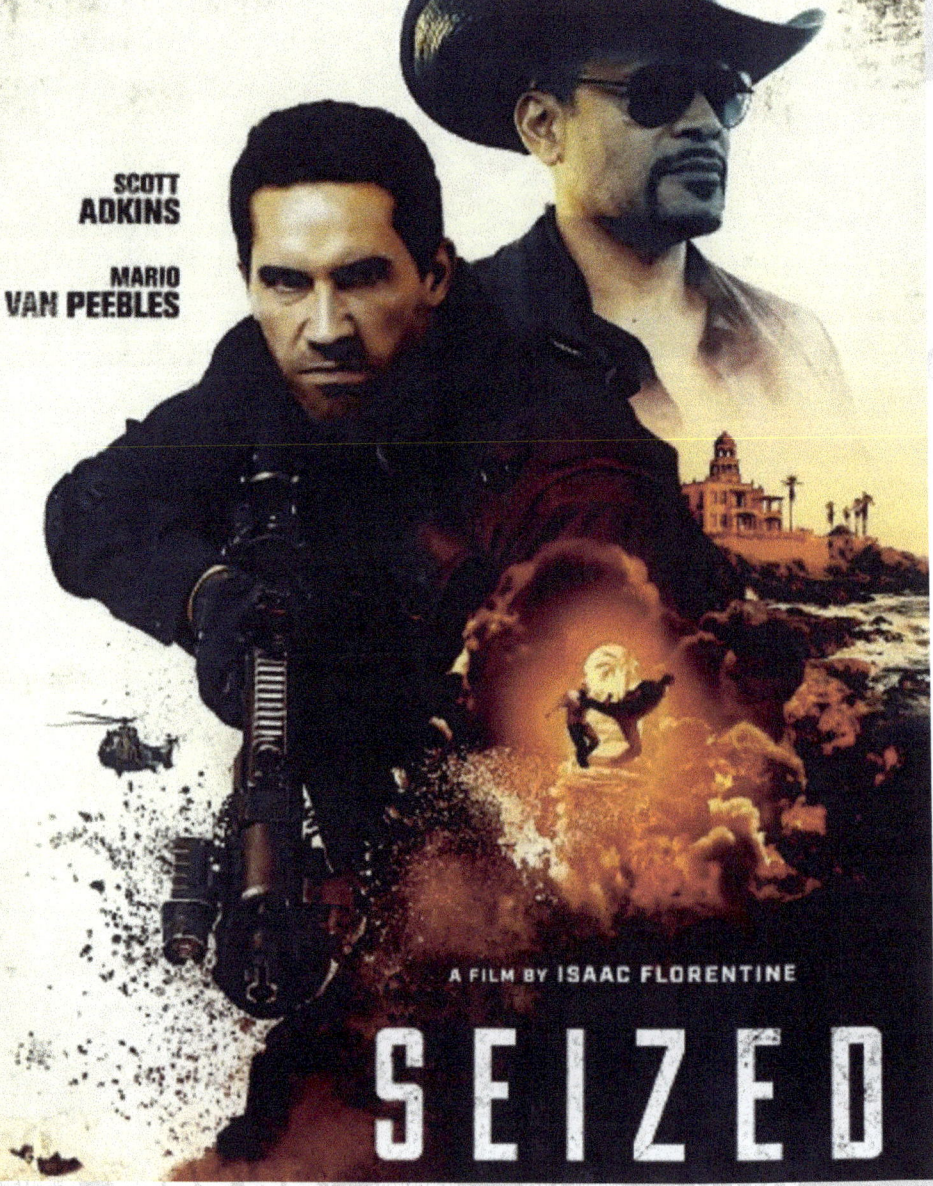

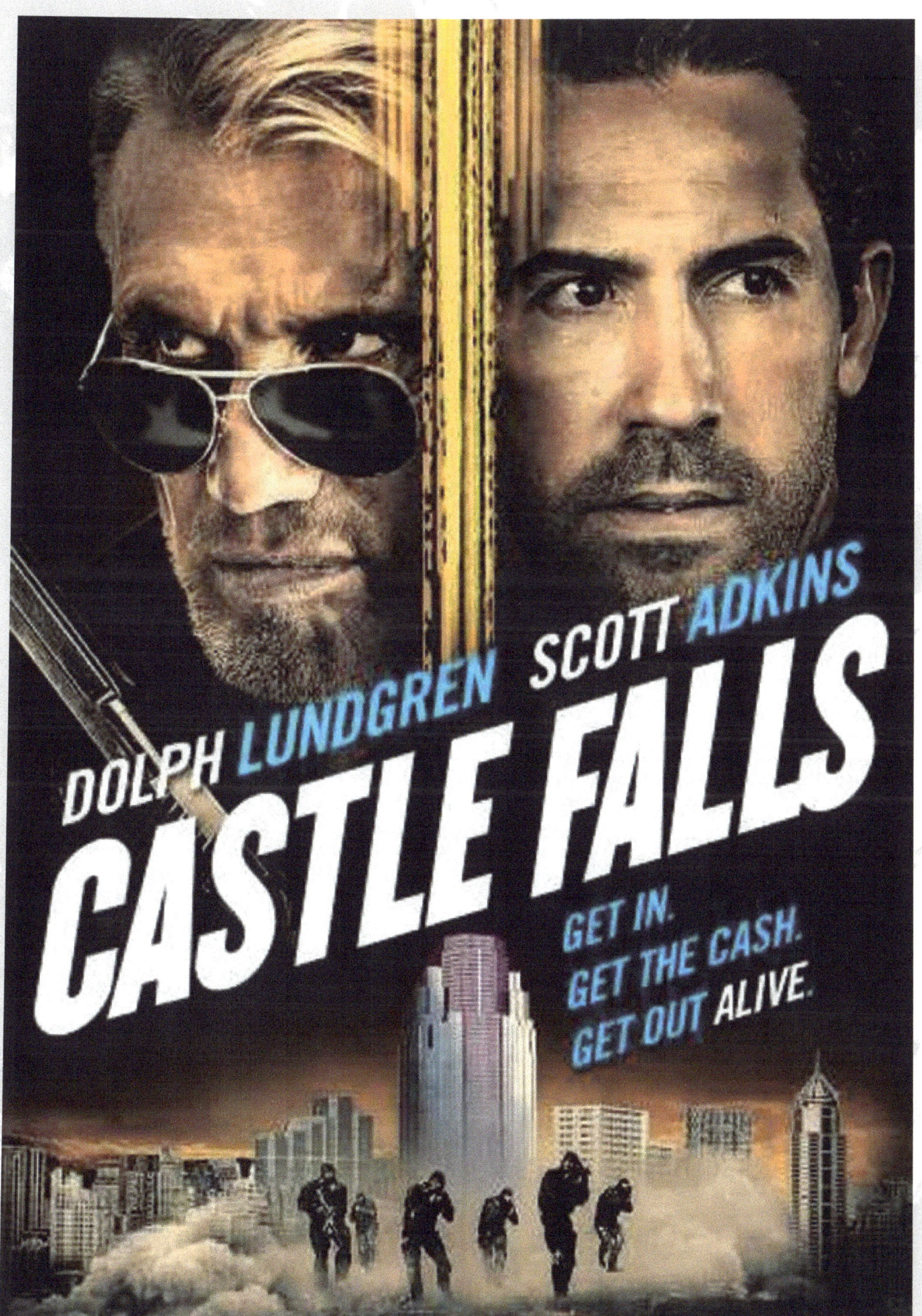

UNDISPUTED III:
REDEMPTION

DUSTIN NGUYEN
AND SCOTT ADKINS
ZERO
TOLERANCE
THEY KILLED HIS ANGEL.
TIME TO UNLEASH HELL.

ADKINS
THE EXPENDABLES 2
SUMMER

SCOTT ADKINS
LEGACY OF LIES

ADKINS
UNIVERSAL SOLDIER
DAY OF RECKONING

SCOTT ADKINS
SAVAGE DOG

TONY JAA
TIGER CHEN
IKO UWAIS
SCOTT ADKINS
MICHAEL JAI WHITE
TRIPLE
THREAT

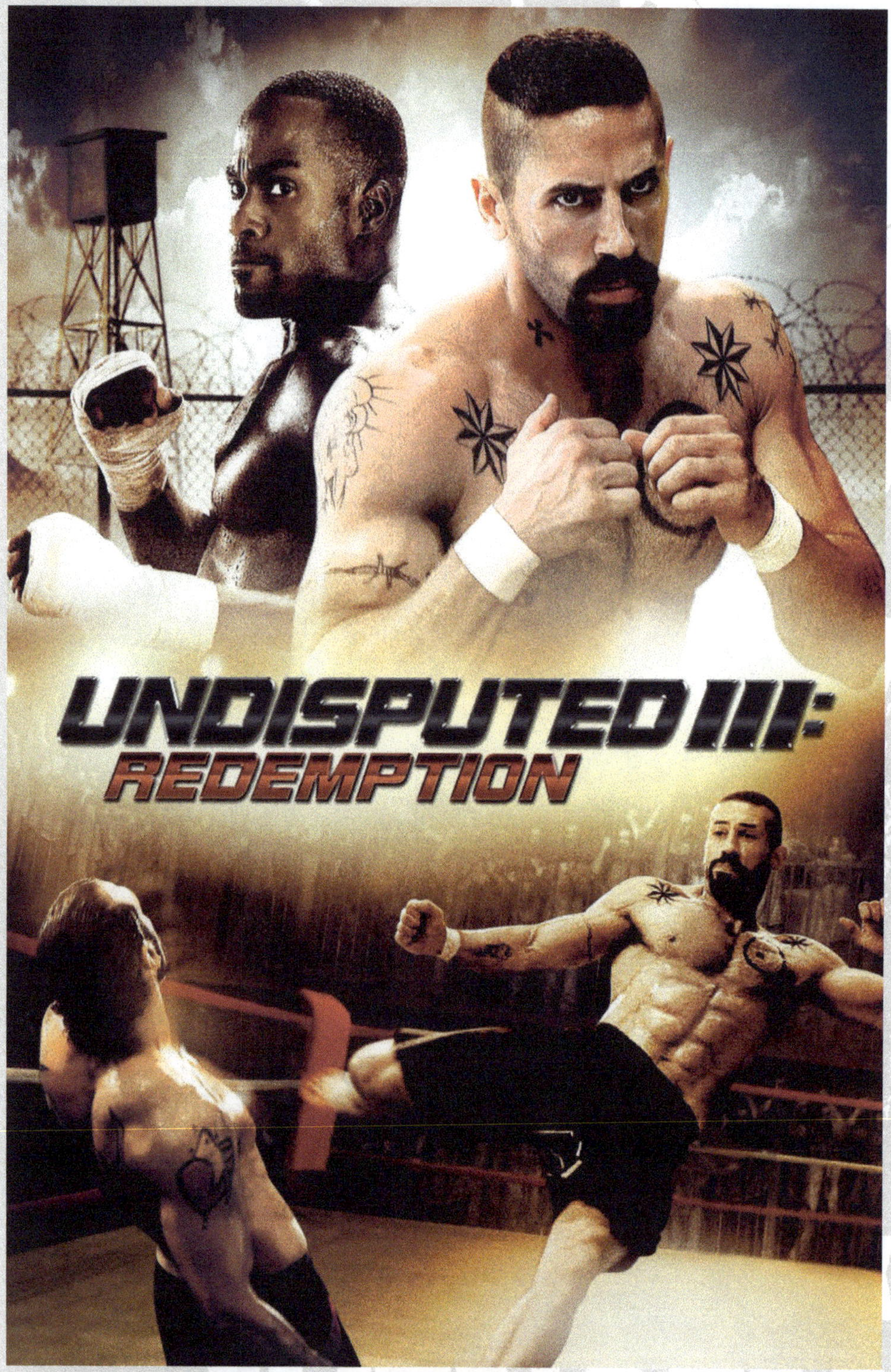

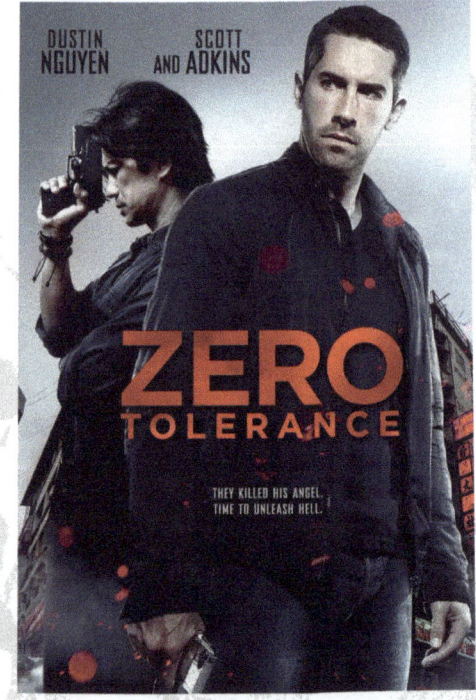

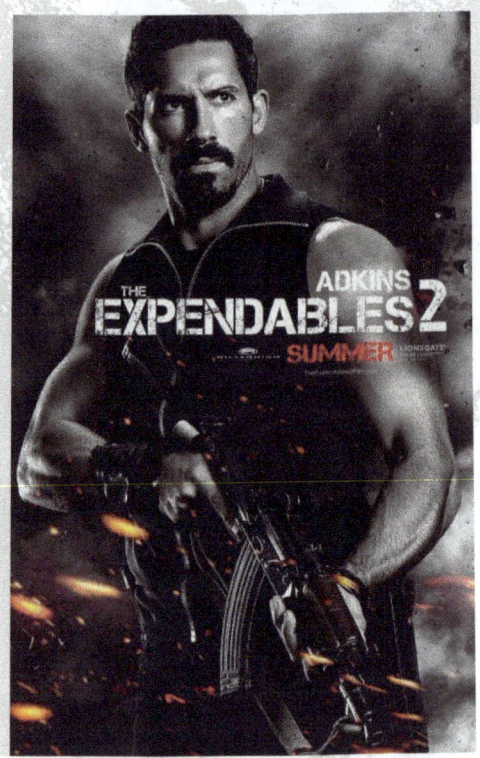

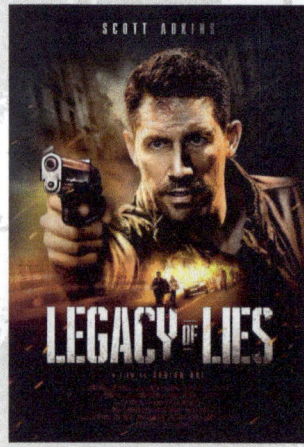

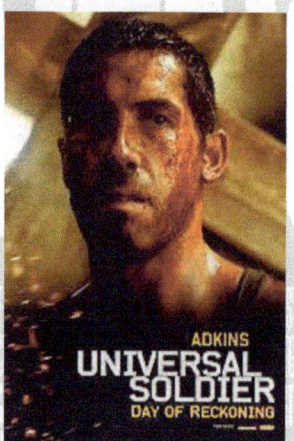

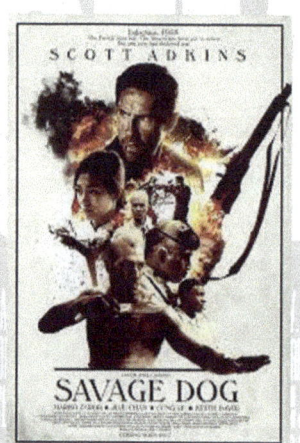

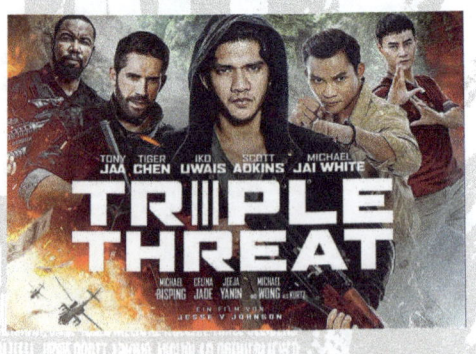

BEAU FOWLER

Interview By Rick Baker

Behind the Scenes with Beau Fowler: Award-Winning Actor, Writer, and Director Talks Career and Latest Projects, Including his Acclaimed role as Poco the Clown in Accident man 2

It is my pleasure to introduce Beau Fowler, a talented actor, writer, and director who has made a name for himself in the entertainment industry. Beau is recognized for his outstanding performance as Poco the Killer Clown in the action-packed film 'Accident Man: Hitman's Holiday' and for his portrayal of Pigtails in the widely popular comedy series 'Code 404'.

In addition to his acting prowess, Beau is also an accomplished writer and director. His short film 'Express Delivery' has received critical acclaim and garnered an impressive 47 awards. However, it is his work on the multi-award-winning action thriller short film 'RED' that truly showcases his creative talents. The film, which Beau wrote and starred in, has received 15 'Best Actor' and 21 'Best Film' awards on the festival circuit and is currently being developed into a feature film.

I had the opportunity to sit down with Beau to discuss his career and the projects that have brought him success in the entertainment industry.

RB: Allow me to begin by asking about the movies you grew up with. It's evident that you enjoy martial arts movies since you visited my Kung Fu cafe when I showed Alan Canvan's "Game of Death Redux" in 2018.

BF: When I was very young, my dad had recorded "Bruce Lee" movies from TV, so I watched them along with old 80's trailers. This was before they removed the Nunchaku scenes from "Enter the Dragon". I consider myself quite lucky to have had the opportunity to watch these movies with my dad. Essentially, I grew up with Hong Kong Cinema, watching predominantly action movies with actors such as Jackie Chan and Donnie Yen. I also watched some comedy movies featuring Steven Chow and, of course, movies directed by John Woo.

RB: I had not such a great choice in my younger days, there was no video and I had to try many times to get into the cinema to watch X-certificate films being under age. And it was not until I moved to London that I began to go to the late night cinema in Leicester Square were I happened upon "Eastern Condors" and that then lead to me creating "Eastern Heroes" Magazine. I was already running an unofficial "Jackie Chan fan Club" when I arrived in London but it was this movie that made me want to showcase other martial art movie talents "Like Sammo Hung, Donnie yen and Yuen bio.

RB: In my younger days, I didn't have a great selection of movies to choose from. Since there were no videos available, I had to make several attempts to sneak into cinemas to watch X-certificate films despite being underage. It wasn't until I moved to London and started going to late-night cinemas in Leicester Square that I stumbled upon "Eastern Condors," which led to the creation of "Eastern Heroes" Magazine. I was already running an unofficial "Jackie Chan fan Club" when I arrived London, but it was this movie that inspired me to showcase other martial arts talents, like Sammo Hung, Donnie Yen, and Yuen Biao and upgrade the fan club to its current format of a "Hong Kong Film magazine".

BF: My friend knew someone who would obtain laserdiscs and transfer them to video, resulting in movies of slightly better quality. As a result, we had a wider selection of films that were not available at the video store

RB: So how did you get into actually doing martial arts was this because of the movies?

BF: I wasn't aware at the time, but my father had studied martial arts, and I only learned about it later in my life. It was actually my father who took me to my first karate class when I was just six years old, even though the requirement was to be eight. At the time, I was quite skinny and small, and the next size up in the class was twice my size. Despite this, the Master allowed me to train there for a few years. It was around that time that I became interested in "Ninja Turtles" and Hong Kong Cinema, which motivated me to start training myself for several years.

Although I was passionate about martial arts, my dad was a photographer, and he had a studio with a punch bag where I used to spend a lot of time practicing as a kid. He also had a pair of wooden nunchakus there, and I remember sneaking them home, watching Bruce Lee using them, and trying to copy his moves through a lot of practice. However, it was the movies that definitely had a big influence on me growing up, and I even dabbled in "capoeira" for a bit.

RB: Wow! Capoeira now that is a difficult style to master, I mean you got to be very flexible and athletic to pull some of those moves off.

BF: You do need lot of agility with the movement, but I loved it. It was great fun. After that, I got into Parkour. A lot of the people around me were practicing different systems, mostly Ninjitsu or Taekwondo. Also, around that time, The Gracie Brothers' Brazilian Jujitsu was becoming very popular. Although I was not following that or watching the tournaments, I enjoyed what I was learning. This certainly helped my growth, and the way it expressed itself on film was a big influence on me growing up.

It's not that you need a lot of agility with the movement, but I loved it. It was great fun. After that, I got into Parkour. A lot of the people around me were practicing different systems, mostly Ninjitsu or Taekwondo. Also, around that time, The Gracie Brothers' Brazilian Jujitsu was becoming very popular. Although I was not following that or watching the tournaments, I enjoyed what I was learning. This certainly helped my growth, and the way it expressed itself on film was a big influence on me growing up.

BF: However, I later started doing southern Shaolin, which I found to be a much deeper system. After studying martial arts for most of my life and finding my new Sifu, it was almost like going back to my childhood. He was on another level, and his knowledge and wisdom were so deep that I was forever a student when training with him.

RB: The same happened to me. Growing up, I tried many martial arts styles, but it was not until later in life, when I started studying Qi Gong, that I found a style that I really enjoyed. When we invited the Grandmaster for a two-hour seminar, I was asked to demonstrate a basic move. However, I was interrupted, and he made a few minor adjustments to my hand and wrists. Suddenly, I felt the energy flowing through me like I had not experienced before. I wanted so badly to pack my bags and go study with him in China (laughing).

BF: Definitely, I think there is a lot of deep routed tradition that seems lost today, and the people learning martial arts today as long as they are gaining something from it then that are good, but I feel that in some systems there is a lot of loss today over a period of time.

RB: The same happened to me. Growing up, I tried many martial arts styles, but it was not until later in life, when I started studying Qi Gong, that I found a style that I really enjoyed. When we invited the Grandmaster for a two-hour seminar, I was asked to demonstrate a basic move. However, I was

interrupted, and he made a few minor adjustments to my hand and wrists. Suddenly, I felt the energy flowing through me like I had not experienced before. I wanted so badly to pack my bags and go study with him in China (laughing). Are you still training?

BF: Although I still keep in shape, these days, I am a terrible student, and I will be going back soon. As an actor, director, and filmmaker, I have had to prioritize these commitments. However, to study martial arts properly, you really have to give up everything else and make that your discipline.

RB: Have you noticed the abundance of people with show reels on platforms such as YouTube and other social media? Some of them are very talented and showcase impressive moves and stunts. However, these skills are only useful if one aims to become a stunt performer or an extra in a fight scene. When people ask me for advice, although I am not the best person to provide pointers, I suggest investing in acting classes to improve their chances of advancing their career and potentially earning speaking roles. Being able to act and fight will give them an edge in a competitive industry.

BF: To be honest, I find a lot of action films boring. However, when I was a kid and in my early twenties, I was always excited to see the next action film and marvel at what they did. For me, most of the action films coming out of Hong Kong were amazing! These days, though, what matters most to me is story and character. Whether you're writing, acting, or directing, it should be about telling a great story with memorable characters.

I see some people trying to bring back the golden age of Hong Kong movies in terms of certain styles or pushing the boundaries of what we can do, and that's fine. However, to have substance in a film, the action has to serve the story and the characters. If you have a film where the action is just there to get you to the next set piece, it can make the movie very disjointed. Even if a scene looks great on screen, it takes away from what you're trying to achieve. Personally, I am no longer

connected to the movie if it's just about showing how cool you can look in that scene. What I'm looking for in a movie is a good story with well-developed character

RB: I must admit, I view films differently now than I did when I was younger. Back then, it was all about the action and the final fight scene. Let's take Bruce Lee, for example. If he had lived, after the success of "Enter the Dragon," Warner Brothers would have given him a blank check for his next movie, and it probably would have been martial arts-driven. However, what we have to remember is that Bruce was an actor before he became a martial artist. I believe that he would have been more attracted to acting roles with action in the movie. But, in general, kung Fu films are not the top box office hits. They do better on video. If Bruce had wanted to continue his success, he would have needed to pitch himself more like Steve McQueen. For instance, take Jackie Chan. His most successful films, like "Rush Hour," were comedy action films, not period kung Fu movies. Today, we see movies like "John Wick" becoming the style to get big audiences. Even in the new one, we have Donnie Yen and Scott Adkins, but it's not just their ability to fight that makes them appealing; it's their performances as well. Bruce Lee was a forward thinker, and he would not want to have been labelled just a kung Fu movie star. That really limits you. Besides, it's hard to keep performing at the level he could when he was 32 without a lot of stunt doubles as he got older.

BF: Indeed, Bruce Lee was very driven by philosophy. I feel that this was just as important to him, if not more important, than martial arts. He wanted to express his philosophy through his martial arts in the most pure way possible, and this was probably what drove him the most, in addition to his dedication to martial arts.

RB: so let's talk about your acting career; because your performance was excellent as "Poco the Clown" what is your back ground I am going to presume you took up acting classes? And who were your influences?

BF: I grew up watching movies and was very interested in all elements of acting, writing, and directing. My main influence growing up was Chow Yun Fat, particularly his acting and on-screen presence. The films he did with John Woo are very iconic. Also, in "City on Fire," he was phenomenal, and Ringo Lam's direction was excellent. I had been acting since I was young, doing all the school plays. I was very keen to start making films, so I saved up by washing cars and bought my first Hi-8 camera when I was 15. I just started shooting homemade films, and part of that was with my sister, who is a great screenwriter and actress. She may go back to acting as she has a great portfolio behind her. We used to shoot little short films, so I was always either shooting or acting, and that just got me deeper and deeper into film. I also studied books and Meisner, and a lot of my friends were also actors, so I could get into deep conversations with them. Getting experience through what I was doing really helped. As a writer, breaking down scenes builds your motivation as an actor.

RB: So let's talk about your role in Accident man 2. Now I believe you got called in at the last moment due to the other actor getting covid, and he had to go isolate in his hotel room, so I guess covid worked In your advantage giving you a great opportunity to step in.

BF: I was approached about two months before production began with an earlier draft of the script, which gave me the essence of the character "Poco" and a good idea of the direction I would take the character. At that stage, a few complications were occurring and I thought I probably wasn't going to get the part of the movie. However, I received a call very late informing me that they wanted me to come over as the person they had cast was in isolation with COVID. I received the script late Saturday night, and so Sunday was a full day of reading my lines and preparing for the part. This was followed by a Zoom call with Scott and the "Kirbys," during which Scott had a very specific idea of how he perceived "Poco" as a new character that was not in the original comic. They had decided with the writer to bring some new elements to the script. However, the "Kirbys" had a different idea for this character, and I realized that my idea for

"Poco" was different again. I talked them through it and let them hear my thoughts, but the fact that he could not feel pain was still a defining characteristic for everyone. This was the turning point for me. Looking at clowns as modern-day jesters, I did some research and discovered that they were smart and always wanted to challenge the system. There were a lot of interesting things I could bring to the character, and I wanted to try to let the audience see that there was something behind "Poco." Often, when clowns are meant to be bringing joy, it is often at the detriment to them. By speaking the truth when he is confronting Scott, and Scott calling him "a liar," this caused him pain inside."

RB: When I watched the film, I thought Scott was very generous with the cast, allowing each character to have their own action piece and showcase their talents. This is great for actors, as having a meaty role to add to their CV is always a plus, as opposed to some films where screen time can be less than 30 seconds. Although all the set pieces were great from the cast, I particularly liked "Poco," and I really wish I knew his backstory and maybe some flashbacks would have enhanced his character more, similar to what we see in the Batman movies with the Joker.

Even though this film is based on a comic strip and "Poco" was something I would have expected to see in a DC comic, I felt there could have been a whole film about him, taking us to the point where we find ourselves in this movie challenging Scott's character. This way, we might have found more empathy for "Poco."

I did mention to Scott that you were a good choice for the role, as you can not only fight, but he can act as well. I'm curious, how much did they take your views on the character, did they say 'we love your ideas, let's do it

BF: As I mentioned earlier, there were two factors to consider regarding the appearance of "Poco" at the Sunday meeting. I briefly explained my thought process on the character to them, and they appeared to enjoy it. This gave me some time to prepare for the character, so I continued working on it while on the plane and in my hotel on Monday. I even came up with a theme tune for him, as the script indicated that he should have one when he entered. I wrote and sang the theme tune Like (Dennis Waterman me jumping in with a British) joke during my flight, and they really liked it when I presented it to them.

I also suggested some changes to a few of Poco's lines, which they approved of, allowing me to incorporate my ideas into the script. Due to my late arrival, I had no real rehearsal time and was only able to watch a video of the fight scene's preview. Therefore, I focused on Poco's journey and his motivation for his actions. During the scene with the baseball bat, I was originally supposed to head-butt Scott, but we decided to make it more comedic. Instead, I honked his nose (parp) and added a more clown-like feel to the moment, which made it more light-hearted

RB: I did laugh at that scene. I mean, clowns often evoke both sadness and humour, and in this case, it worked particularly well, especially with the audience I watched it with. The scene helped break the tension, which would have been difficult to achieve in other scenes.

BF: Scott really enjoyed the scene where I slapped him on the face and pinched his nose. They were kind enough to allow me to have some input, so I discussed my ideas with George, who was directing that scene while Harry was working on another fight sequence. I collaborated with George on my suggestions for that scene, but I also had an idea for when Poco gets his neck broken. I proposed that we bring back the theme tune that Poco sang when he first appeared.

RB: **To be honest I really would have liked him to have live so he could come back in the third part or have his own movie (LOL) but to be perfectly honest I loved your performance as "Poco" and I thought you did as well as another A-list actor could have done honestly**

BF: Well thank you for that Rick, I really appreciate that`

RB: **Considering the background and the limited time you had to create and deliver the character, it was extraordinary how well you portrayed "Poco" on screen. The advantage of wearing a mask is that you are not typecast for future roles because no one can recognize you. I imagine that wearing a mask and full clown getup would also help you develop the character further. Typically, actors stay in character when rehearsing for weeks, but you had just two days, which is a real testament to your abilities**

BF: As a clown, you really have to exaggerate your character. Therefore, I didn't get much sleep, but I hope that my performance will appear more organic on screen.

RB: **who came up for the look of the clown? And it looked great fun making Accident man 2**

BF: They had a general idea of how they wanted Poco to look, and I suggested a few ideas. We discussed whether to show him with a bit of stubble showing through the makeup or have him come out clean. The good thing was that on the day of shooting, I could keep the makeup on without having to go through the process of having it put on time and time again. It took about two to two and a half hours to apply the

makeup in the morning and another couple of hours at the end of the day. And yes I am very grateful for Scott giving me the opportunity, and it was a great experience working alongside the Kirby Brothers too and the rest of the cast great experience or me.

RB: **Well Beau we could talk for hours mainly because I loved this character, and I think you Scott and the team made a really good comedy action film that was really lapped up by the audience when it was screened in London, I am convinced that there is some great thongs coming your way in 2023 and as an when the do I will be back knocking on your door for another interview, thank you so much for taking time out and lets catch up again soon.**

BF: pleasure Rick look forward to reading the article

UNLEASHING THE POWER OF SCOTT ADKINS

I have carefully selected five Scott Adkins films that I would highly recommend to any new follower of his work. With a vast catalogue of movies and a career that has gone from strength to strength in the past two decades, Scott has produced many films that I have thoroughly enjoyed. While most people reading this issue may have already seen his work, I always like to think that a new generation of action fans is discovering the genre around the world. Therefore, I consider it a great opportunity to expand people's interests and introduce them to Scott Adkins, who I believe is one of the biggest talents to have hit our screens in recent years. It's even more thrilling that he is a local lad from the Midlands, just like me. Thus, this guide offers a selection of my top five "desert island" Scott Adkins movies, if I had to choose just five.

AVENGEMENT (2019)

"Avengement" is a gritty and action-packed revenge thriller, featuring martial arts expert Scott Adkins in one of his most intense and captivating performances to date. Directed by Jesse V. Johnson, the film tells the story of Cain Burgess (Adkins), a skilled fighter who is wrongfully imprisoned for a crime he didn't commit. During his time behind bars, Cain is brutally beaten and scarred by his fellow inmates, leading him to become a hardened and vengeful man determined to seek retribution against those who betrayed him.

One of the film's greatest strengths is Adkins' performance as Cain. Adkins brings a level of depth and complexity to the character, portraying him as a man with a tragic past who is consumed by his need for revenge. He delivers a powerhouse performance, showcasing his incredible physical abilities as a martial artist while also displaying a range of emotional nuances that make Cain a fully realized and compelling protagonist.

The action sequences in "Avengement" are simply stunning. The film is chock-full of thrilling fight scenes that are expertly choreographed and executed with precision and intensity. Adkins, along with a talented ensemble cast of fellow martial artists, brings a level of authenticity and realism to the fights that make them all the more impactful and exhilarating to watch.

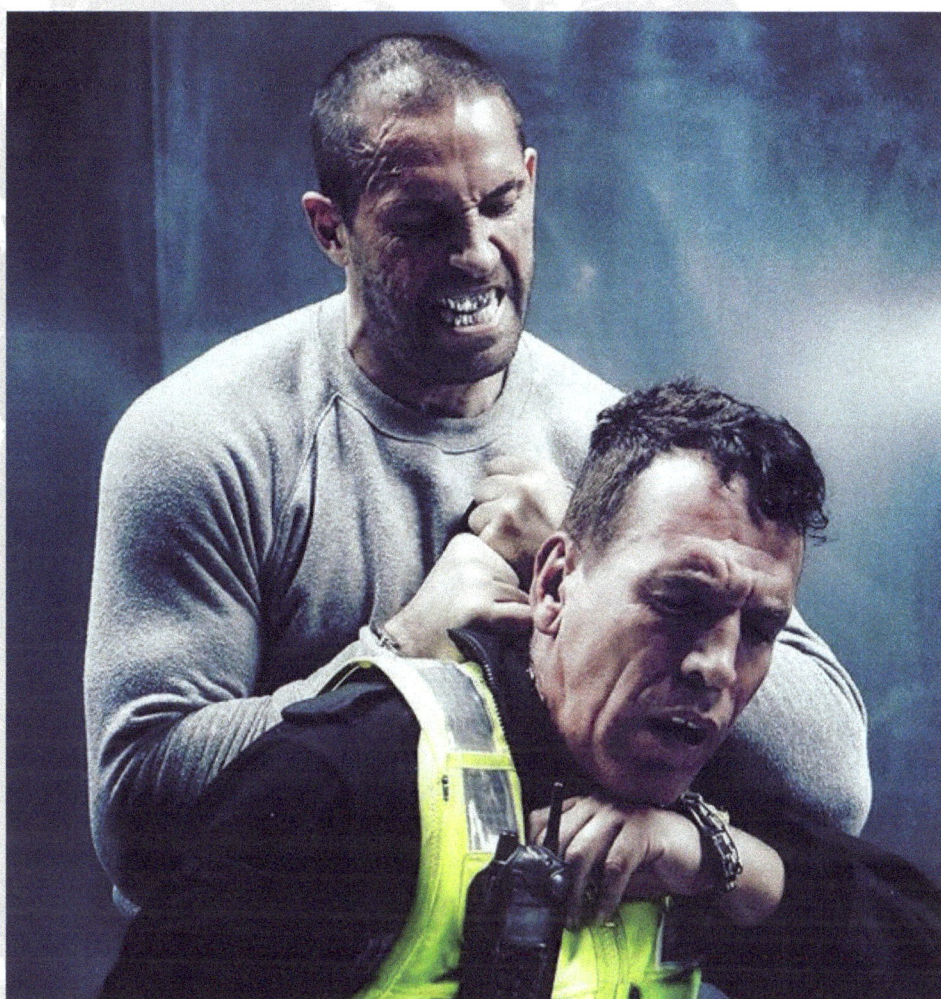

The supporting cast, which includes actors like Craig Fairbrass and Thomas Turgoose, also deliver strong performances, with each bringing a distinct personality and flavor to their respective characters.

"Avengement" is a dark and gritty film, but it also has a surprising amount of heart. As the story unfolds, we learn more about Cain's past and the events that led him to become the man he is today. This backstory adds a layer of emotional weight to the film and makes Cain's journey all the more poignant and resonant.

Overall, "Avengement" is a must-see for fans of action cinema, especially those who appreciate martial arts and fight choreography. With its incredible action, strong performances, and compelling story, it's a standout film in Scott Adkins' impressive filmography.

IP MAN 4: THE FINALE

Ip Man 4: The Finale" is a thrilling and emotional conclusion to the legendary martial arts series, featuring a standout performance by Scott Adkins as the film's primary antagonist. Directed by Wilson Yip, the film sees Donnie Yen return to the iconic role of Wing Chun grandmaster Ip Man, who travels to San Francisco to help his star pupil, Bruce Lee, establish a martial arts school.

Adkins shines as the film's villain, a U.S. Marine named Barton Geddes, who is determined to prove the superiority of American martial arts over Chinese martial arts. Adkins brings his trademark intensity and physicality to the role, portraying Geddes as a formidable and ruthless adversary. His fight scenes with Yen are among the film's highlights, with the two martial artists delivering a series of breath-taking battles that showcase their incredible skills.

Yen is also excellent in his return as Ip Man, bringing a sense of gravitas and stoicism to the character. The film explores the themes of legacy and tradition that have been central to the series, as Ip Man struggles to pass on his knowledge and philosophy to a new generation while also dealing with personal struggles and the challenges of being a foreigner in America.

The supporting cast also delivers strong performances, with actors like Vanness Wu and Wu Yue providing memorable turns as Ip Man's allies. The film's themes of cultural exchange and mutual respect between different martial arts traditions provide a message of unity and collaboration that feels particularly timely and resonant.

Of course, as with all films in the series, the action in "Ip Man 4: The Finale" is a major highlight. The film features some of the most thrilling and inventive fight scenes in the series, with Yen and Adkins leading an incredibly talented ensemble cast of martial artists. The fight choreography is expertly executed and seamlessly integrated into the story, resulting in a film that is both visually stunning and emotionally engaging.

Overall, "Ip Man 4: The Finale" is a must-watch for fans of martial arts and action cinema. With its excellent performances, powerful themes, and thrilling action, it's a fitting conclusion to the series and a standout entry in Scott Adkins' already impressive filmography.

ONE SHOT (2021)

"One Shot" is a thrilling and action-packed martial arts film featuring the incomparable Scott Adkins in the lead role. Directed by James Nunn, the film follows Adkins' character, James, a former soldier with a troubled past who finds himself caught in the middle of a deadly conspiracy.

Adkins once again proves himself to be a powerhouse performer, bringing his signature blend of incredible physical abilities and emotional depth to the role of James. As the character becomes embroiled in a dangerous game of cat and mouse, Adkins conveys a palpable sense of desperation and determination, making James a relatable and sympathetic protagonist.

The action sequences in "One Shot" are a sight to behold. The film features some of the most impressive fight scenes in recent memory, with Adkins and his co-stars executing stunning choreography with breathtaking skill and precision. The film's action is both stylish and visceral, providing non-stop thrills from start to finish.

The supporting cast also delivers strong performances, with actors like Ashley Greene and Ryan Phillippe bringing a level of gravitas and intensity to their roles. The film's villains are suitably menacing and intimidating, providing a formidable challenge for James and adding an extra layer of tension to the proceedings.

As with many of Adkins' films, "One Shot" is a movie that is made with a deep appreciation for the martial arts genre. The film pays homage to classic action cinema while also injecting its own unique energy and style. The result is a film that is both a love letter to the genre and a standout example of its own.

"One Shot" is a must-watch for fans of martial arts and action cinema. With its incredible fight scenes, strong performances, and pulse-pounding action, it's a film that will keep you on the edge of your seat from beginning to end. Scott Adkins once again proves himself to be one of the genre's most talented and exciting stars, making "One Shot" a standout entry in his already impressive filmography.

UNDISPUTED 2: LAST MAN STANDING (2002)

Undisputed 2: Last Man Standing" is a thrilling and action-packed martial arts film that solidified Scott Adkins' status as one of the genre's most talented and charismatic stars. Directed by Isaac Florentine, the film is a sequel to the 2002 film "Undisputed" and sees Adkins take on the role of Yuri Boyka, a ruthless and skilled fighter in a Russian prison.

Adkins is simply electric in the role of Boyka, bringing a sense of ferocity and intensity to the character that makes him impossible to ignore. The actor's incredible physical abilities are on full display in the film's numerous fight scenes, which are expertly choreographed and executed with breath-taking precision and power. Adkins' charisma and magnetism as an actor also make Boyka a compelling and memorable protagonist, despite his villainous tendencies.

The film's story is engaging and well-crafted, as Boyka navigates a world of corruption and deceit in order to earn his freedom and prove his worth as a fighter. The supporting cast, including Michael Jai White as boxer George Chambers, also delivers strong performances, with each character adding a unique perspective and personality to the story.

Of course, the film's action is a major highlight. The fight scenes in "Undisputed 2" are some of the most memorable and

exciting in recent martial arts cinema, with Adkins and his co-stars executing complex and thrilling choreography that leaves a lasting impression. The film's fight scenes are brutal and intense, but also expertly crafted and visually stunning, making them a true highlight of the film.

Overall, "Undisputed 2: Last Man Standing" is a must-watch for fans of martial arts and action cinema. With its incredible performances, engaging story, and stunning action, it's a standout film in Scott Adkins' impressive filmography, and a worthy successor to the original "Undisputed

BOYKA: UNDISPUTED (2006)

Boyka: Undisputed" is a visceral and emotionally charged martial arts film that showcases Scott Adkins at the top of his game. Directed by Todor Chapkanov with Isaac Florentine producing, the film sees Adkins' character, Yuri Boyka, on a mission to right a terrible wrong after accidentally killing an opponent in the ring.

Adkins once again delivers a powerhouse performance as Boyka, bringing both physicality and emotional depth to the character. The film's fight scenes are some of the most thrilling and well-executed in the franchise, with Adkins' impressive martial arts skills on full display. However, it's the film's emotional arc that sets it apart from its predecessors. Boyka is shown as not just a formidable fighter, but a man grappling with guilt and a desire to make things right, giving the character a sense of depth and humanity that is both compelling and relatable.

The supporting cast is also strong, with the film's villains providing a formidable challenge for Boyka to overcome. The story is engaging and well-crafted, with the stakes raised high as Boyka risks everything to save the widow of the fighter he accidentally killed.

Overall, "Boyka: Undisputed" is a standout entry in the franchise and one of Scott Adkins' best films to date. The film's action sequences are adrenaline-fueled and expertly

crafted, but it's the emotional resonance of the story that makes it truly special. With its themes of sacrifice and atonement, "Boyka: Undisputed" is a powerful and memorable film that is sure to satisfy fans of martial arts and action cinema. Here's hoping that either the pitched "Undisputed" TV series or "Undisputed 5" in movie form will get off the ground to give audiences another chance to see Boyka in action.

INTERVIEW WITH ANDY LONG
STUNTMAN EXTRORDINAIRE
By Rick Baker

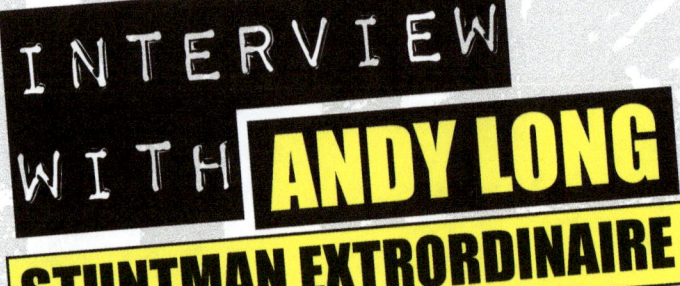

Andy Long, also known as Andreas Ngyuen, is an accomplished actor and stuntman with an impressive career in the film industry. Born in Vietnam, he spent his formative years in Germany, where he discovered his love for martial arts at a young age. Andy was particularly inspired by the legendary Jackie Chan, and he set his sights on emulating his hero's success in action filmmaking.

Determined to achieve his dreams, Andy devoted himself to mastering the art of stunt work and independent filmmaking. His unwavering focus and dedication eventually led him to Paris, France, where he finally had the opportunity to meet Jackie Chan in person. This meeting proved to be a life-changing experience for Andy, as it only served to further ignite his passion for the world of action movies.

Over the course of his career, Andy has worked on a wide variety of films and television shows, earning a reputation as a skilled and versatile performer. He has established himself as a prominent figure in the world of action cinema, and his passion for the craft is evident in every project he takes on.

With a wealth of experience and a deep understanding of the art of filmmaking, Andy Long continues to push the boundaries of what is possible in the world of action entertainment. His impressive body of work stands as a testament to his talent, dedication, and unyielding determination to succeed.

RB: Hi Andy, thank you for taking the time to chat with me. Let me dive straight in and ask for some background information. What led you to the film industry? Was it your

love of Hong Kong films or your experience as a practicing martial artist that motivated you to take your skills to the big screen and reach the next level?

AL: Well, first and foremost, it was Hong Kong cinema. Those movies were always present in my family home, mainly because Chinese movies were the only films that were dubbed in Vietnamese. My parents watched these movies because Vietnam did not have that market at the time, so they searched out the ones that were dubbed. As a result, I quickly became very familiar with these movies. Since we had no local video shop to rent or watch these movies, we relied on copies from friends or relatives recorded on two VHS tapes (RB: I know what you mean, laughing). I managed to get hold of a bunch of movies, but to be honest; my true love was always Jackie Chan

RB: So what were the first Jackie Chan films you saw that made him stand out from the rest?

AL: Because I was so young, I cannot remember which film introduced me to Jackie Chan's work. At that time, I wasn't allowed to watch the "Police Story" movies, as they were considered too violent for me at such a young age. However, I was allowed to watch kung fu movies, so "Drunken Master" and "Snake in the Eagle's Shadow" were the ones that I enjoyed very much.

RB: Yes, for me, I loved the early traditional movies, particularly "Snake and Crane Arts of Shaolin". I think Jackie was at his physical peak in this movie. I remember seeing him do a head spring with his arms behind his back on the stomach of one of the guys when fighting the three fishermen by the lake. This was just a throwaway moment for Jackie, but it was something you never see. Because Jackie had more control over the action, he could really push his abilities to the limit. But remember Jackie was straight out of the peaking opera school his class was like the last tier before it closed down

AL: I really wish I had been alive when that school was open (smile). Unfortunately, Kung Fu classes were not available where I lived, and perhaps my parents could not afford to send me, as the lessons may have only been available to private students. At that time, there was nothing I really wanted to learn that was on offer in my area. When I attended my first student class at the age of six, I started to make things up like I saw in the movies. However, the class did not teach me those moves. So, I tried to practice the things I saw in the movies in my backyard. At that time, what I was doing was not "Parkour," but I called it "Jackie Chan Jumping." I would jump around on and off things. Later on, I was invited to return to my Judo classes as they would let me practice on their mats. I thought that was fine, as I could now do

Page 47 Accident Man: Hitman's Holiday

the things I was trying outside and have the safety of the mats. This was an opportunity for me to self-teach myself Kung Fu moves and acrobatics.

RB: Did you manage to find a gymnastics school to help you with your acrobatics?

AL: Well, because back then these schools would have been expensive, I was actually self-teaching myself. My guide was watching Hong Kong movies and admiring the screen fighting. This was my inspiration for training.

RB: For me growing up I was very much influenced by "Bruce Lee" I discovered Jackie in the 80's and started my company in 1988 the same year you was born (Laughing) but you also must have been watching Bruce Lee films as well.

AL: Yes, my father liked the Bruce Lee films. I remember watching "Way of the Dragon." Actually, my father went to see "Big Boss" in the theatre with my mum when it played. So, I saw them and liked them. But for me, it was always Jackie Chan that was my influence. I liked his personality in the movies, and I did not think of myself as a tough guy. I liked the way Jackie would play the underdog, and I could identify with this character. This is why I loved watching him so much. Although I enjoyed watching the other characters, I could identify best with Jackie Chan.

RB: While you were practicing and learning these skills, did you think to yourself, "I want to learn these skills because I want to do the movies?" Or were you simply enjoying copying your hero? I'm not sure if you told your mum and dad that you wanted to make Kung Fu movies, they might have laughed and hoped the idea would go away. Your family may have even said, "Go get a proper job."

AL: Yes, (laughing) I think it's the case with all Asian kids that their parents would like them to pursue a traditional profession like becoming a doctor, lawyer, or something similar. However, in my mind, my goal was to be in films. I wanted to be like "Jackie Chan!" and make films as a tribute to him, do stunts, and be as good as Jackie. That

was what was in my mind as I trained.

RB: What would they have liked to see you become?

AL: A doctor or something safe and solid, of course. I mean, right up until recently, they still hoped. But I was sneaking out during my studies to keep focused on my dream. In my mind, my goal was very clear: I wanted to end up in movies, and I wanted to be like Jackie. I was hoping that one day, I could contribute to one of his movies as a stunt member. Even when I look back at my old school books, you can see me drawing and saying, 'I want to be in a Jackie Chan movie.

RB: Well you not what they say? If you think positive and your mind is focused you can achieve your goals.
AL: Yes, also you must pursuit this dream without a plan-B.

RB: So tell me the story how you got into the industry? You have left school, your head id full of Kung Fu movies and Jackie Chan, how did you turn that thought into a reality?

AL: Even though I am younger, the internet was not as readily available to me. However, in 1999, when I watched "Jackie Chan my Stunts," I discovered that it was possible to learn how to make films from a master. I had a Hi-8 camera, which was very valuable to me but also very expensive. I had to secretly take it out of the house to record myself. Initially, I tried to enlist the help of my family members, such as my cousin and brother, but their lack of interest in Kung Fu movies made their efforts less successful than mine. Later, as the internet became more widely available, I was able to connect with others who shared my interest, such as "Eric Jacobus." This led me to form a small team in my hometown of Germany. After finishing school, I traveled to the United States to visit other independent filmmakers, where I had the opportunity to shoot with everyone I met, including your friend "Vlad Rimburg" (Gangs of London 2.

RB: Did you manage to create a show reel to showcase your talents?

AL: Yes, I did! But it can take time to be accepted as someone wanting to copy the Hong Kong style of stunt action back

then especially for the westerners as we all wanted to be work with Jackie Chan.

RB: So when you first started, was it hard to open doors, and did you get many knockbacks?

AL: I experienced many setbacks on my journey to replicate the Hong Kong style of stunts. It seemed like every time I thought I was going to meet people who would encourage me and support me, I was let down. Even people whom I looked up to and believed would tell me I was on the right path ended up telling me the opposite. It's possible that they were motivated by jealousy or a desire to protect me from disappointment if my dreams didn't come true. Interestingly enough, it was often the people I didn't know as well who were the most encouraging. They would tell me, "Of course you're going to make it."

RB: I understand exactly what you mean. I've had similar experiences in my own career, where the people closest to me seemed to try to dissuade me from pursuing my dreams. They believed that they were sparing me from disillusionment and pushing me towards finding a more traditional job. It was actually people whom I hardly knew that provided me with the encouragement and support I needed to keep going. It's funny how that works sometimes. There's a saying that goes, "You can find comfort in conversations with strangers." (Laughs).

AL: It's often strange how the people closest to me would tell me not to pursue my dreams, thinking that they were offering good advice. This made me feel like I was on my own, but it didn't deter me from trying to achieve my ultimate goal of joining the "Jackie Chan Stunt Team." I was still living in Germany at the time and managed to land a few jobs doing stunt work.

RB: So back then in Germany what sort of work were you being offered, TV commercials or movie work?

AL: I was also being offered some smaller projects around that time. One of my biggest jobs was working on a German TV series called "Lasko," where I played the role of a monk. This opportunity allowed me to start doing well and to connect with stunt coordinators. Despite these achievements, I still had my sights set on working with Jackie Chan.

RB: Why did you not just head to Hong Kong at that stage to increase your chances? Like some of my friends did.

AL: At first, I was still in my comfort zone and hesitant to leave due to financial reasons and the fear of not knowing anyone in the new place.

RB: Back in the 80's people I knew would just head to Chungking mansions, because back then the film studios would send people there looking for some cheap labour to be extras or killed, often backpackers needing a few extra bucks for their journey. For some this would lead to them getting regular work.

AL: For me, trying to get into the world of Jackie Chan stunts was like entering another universe. As I started getting more stunt work, I began putting together scenes in the hopes that Jackie would see them. Whenever he was in Europe, I would try to get my show reel in front of him, whether it was at premieres or during interviews, since he was in Europe quite often at that time. One example was during the promotion of "Around the World in Eighty Days" when I was just 14 years old. I wanted to get something to him during his visit, but unfortunately, I was not able to get that close to him. However, I did manage to receive a fan letter from his dialogue coach, Diana Wang, with an autograph from Jackie Chan. She thanked me for offering my services to the team but explained that they needed experienced people and couldn't recruit from everywhere. Nevertheless, she encouraged me to keep pursuing my dreams. I took this as an inspiration to continue following my dreams.

RB: But you were still very young. However Jackie is getting older?

AL: It's true that at the time, my thoughts were the same, so I had to set myself a deadline to get onto "Armour of God 3." I was a big fan of that franchise, so I made it my focus and aimed to be in that movie. Even though my career in Germany was

going well, I decided to turn down every job offer when the shooting for the movie was announced, so that I could work with Jackie Chan. At the time, I had no contacts and knew nothing about the process for joining him. I even reached out to "Willie Chan," who replied but was no longer working with Jackie. By this point, I felt like I was stalking the crew.

I found a Jackie Chan blog that collected information on him, and there was a picture from one of the camera guys that said they were shooting with Tai Gong (Big Brother) in Paris. Without hesitation, I grabbed my backpack and headed to Paris, even though I was already broke from turning down work offers. I only had 50 euros to travel and survive until I met Jackie. I had no idea where they would be shooting, so I wandered around Paris, checking all the sights.

While there, I started emailing French stunt guys for help. Finally, one guy replied and knew they were shooting at a castle for the opening scene of the film. I traveled there and saw all the trailers and crew gathered outside the castle. I had prepared five demo reels, but I wasn't sure how long it would take for me to get kicked off the set. So, I started passing my show reel to the first person I saw. Finally, a stunt team member approached me, and I explained my situation. He walked with me to the catering area and said they had seen everything they needed from me and would call me if they needed me.

I was alone on the set, trying to process what had just happened, when I saw Jackie on a Segway in the distance. Panicking, I checked my bag and realized I only had a little backup copy of my demo reel without a cover. I ran up to him, bowed, and introduced myself as Andy, a stuntman from Germany, and expressed my desire to work with him. I held out my demo tape, and he took it and smiled before riding away.

RB: So let me get this straight, you finally meet your hero for the first time, and instead of asking for an autograph or telling him how much you enjoyed all his movies, you asked for a job. Your heart must have been pounding so much to take it all in within just a few moments.

AL: Of course! Here's a grammatically correct version:

I know it's funny (laughing) that I didn't touch or shake his hand, but meeting him alone without the crowd was such a magical moment for me. It's a moment I will never forget. As they continued shooting, I somehow managed to stay on the set without getting kicked off. I took the opportunity to watch Jackie working and sometimes he would come out and see me standing there. He gave me a thumbs up, and I thought he was treating his fans nicely (laughs). The funny thing is that I didn't leave. I found a place to crash so I could turn up the next day. The whole crew was surprised to see me there and said, "Still here, okay?" Jackie saw me and probably thought, "He's still here, okay!" By this stage, I must have given the impression that I was working there. The French and Hong Kong crews started letting me in and out of the set, saying, "The stunt crew is over there." As I got more established on set, I began offering to help the stunt crews by carrying their bags and equipment. This led to them giving me a few small jobs to do, which carried on for a week. Then Jackie started calling me by my name, and he would say, "Andy, come here and hold this." It was something I had to hold to make sure it didn't get into the frame while they were fighting. I was really enjoying those moments, especially when I got a shoulder tap from Jackie. I believe that this was the key for them to reach out to me again.

By the time they had wrapped up the Paris shoot, one of them told me, "I don't know what you're expecting, as it's not that easy

to just join the team. If we invited you, we would have to train you, so don't have your expectations too high in case it doesn't work out." On one side, I felt disappointed, but on the other side, I still had hope.

RB: But what a great experience people reading this should be inspired by that story that if you follow your dreams they can come true.

AL: It was a magical time for me, and I hope it inspires people with similar thoughts. Afterward, I went home, and in my mind, I confirmed to myself that I had made it, even just to have met Jackie and been on a set with him. I had made him aware of me, and coming home to tell my story was a great feeling.

RB: How did this experience affect you as you walked away from achieving your goal to be on a movie set with Jackie, but unsure of your future? Were you left feeling like this was the end of it, or were you

optimistic that it could be a new beginning?

AL: It was a mix of feelings for me. On one hand, I knew I had achieved something significant by being there because, when I first arrived in Paris, I was questioning myself and wondering what I was doing there. I was praying every day as I had no plan or itinerary, but somehow, I managed to meet Jackie, and that was a real blessing for me. After all those years, I was standing in front of Jackie. But, when the shooting in Paris was finished, it felt like a closure to that moment, and I was left unsure if they would ever call me back. Did I do my best? I didn't know what the future held, but I was grateful for the experience.

RB: Your story is truly inspiring, and it's almost like something you would see in a movie, which often doesn't happen in real life. It reminds me of a young Jet Li in the movie "Shaolin Temple," where he sits outside the temple, just wanting a chance to train inside. Rain, sun, or snow, he doesn't give up, and it's a real underdog story. That's how I perceive what you just told me. It's just like a movie. So Now your back home what happens in the next part of this movie (laughing)

AL: Well, now the next move is no longer in my hands, so it's up to them. They know me now, and I must wait to see if I get a call. They tell me that Jackie has watched my show reel and likes what he saw with my skill sets, they may invite me to see if we can work together. I'm not sure what to expect if they invite me, but I'm keeping my fingers crossed.

RB: So what project would they be inviting you on?

AL: They were still shooting "Armour of God 3: Chinese Zodiac," and they would be shooting the big scenes in Beijing. So, I had to get my visa, and I thought I should be careful about how much I should say about my news. I wanted to show my respect for Jackie and keep this offer under wraps. But when I arrived, they threw me straight in at the deep end with the stunt crew. My only problem was to understand the language, but they would just shout at me until I got what they were saying right (laughs). This, as they say, had to go through the school of hard knocks, and

it was a very difficult time for me. But, learning during this time was also the best experience for me.

RB: How long were you on that shoot for?

AL: In Paris, we shot for approximately two weeks, and in Beijing, we spent almost half a year filming. This was my biggest dream, and I was willing to accept any offer to be there and live my dream. I would have even gone for free (laughs). The most memorable moments were when Jackie joined us after we had completed all the preparation. I enjoyed observing Jackie set up a scene, and he seemed to have eyes in the back of his head as he always knew when I was watching him. For instance, I would be watching him, and he would turn around and say something like, "Hey! First time,in Beijing!" I would stutter a little and reply, "YES."

RB: I think that the people that survive to work with Jackie again, have to be able to keep their head down, and take direction from him, and it's good to study him so you can a feel of the way he works. **So did your being observant and dedicated get you a place in Jackie's Stunt Group?**

AL: I had a feeling that everyone hated me, and I believe Jackie could sense that I was being targeted simply because I wanted to learn as much as possible from him. Jackie was my idol, and his influence on me was enormous, so now that I had this opportunity, I wanted to take full advantage of it. The moment when I felt like I had accomplished something was when I received the second call back to Latvia, and some of the guys who were previously on set were no longer there.

RB: You were invited to go back to Latvia again, and you must have thought that you had made it. You were now accepted as one of Jackie's stunt team members.

AL: I was accepted from the beginning, but somehow, I found myself in competition with other stunt guys, such as some of the China stunt team members who were there for the first time and had to prove themselves to be worthy of the team. However, when we had the second schedule, these guys were not being called back, but I did receive the call

RB: so who now were you doubling for?
Did you do any screen doubling?

AL: Well, I did some doubling, but for about 80% of the time, I was doing the rigging, and this provided me with valuable experience. I had to learn it on the go with the movies. All my life, I had trained in martial arts and stunt doubling, but with Hong Kong movies, the most important thing is the rigging. When we got the chance to perform it, it was very cool for me. You think that what you have learned will see you through all your life, but for me, the special moments were also in the preparation. It's an important skill to have. However, a moment I cannot forget was when I was called, and you hear 3, 2, 1, and there I was staring straight into Jackie's eyes. In those three seconds, the whole of Jackie Chan's movies rolled through my mind. It was one of the most amazing moments of my life.

RB: I had one of those moments

when I was at the London premiere of 'Rumble in the Bronx' at 'Planet Hollywood,' and Jackie was there. His press agents were making it difficult to get close to him, but he saw Toby and me and came over. My heart was pumping as this was my first meeting with Jackie, and I said to him, 'Hi, Jackie, my name is Rick Baker. I am a huge fan, and it's so great to actually meet you.' He replied, 'Yes, yes. I know who you are. Quentin Tarantino says great things about you.' That was my magic moment - Jackie acknowledging me and getting great word-of-mouth for Quentin (**priceless**)

AL: (Laughing) I know, and for me, the moment he hit me, I felt no pain. It has been good for me. I have been in the 'Armour of God' franchise and also the 'Police Story' franchise. When they called me for 'Police Story 2013,' it was different. Working on this movie was totally different from working on 'Armour of God 3.' This was such a big film, and they had a lot more crew, but on 'Police Story,' Jackie had much more time to talk with us about his movies, and it felt very much like we were a family - much more intimate. Film-making-wise, I enjoyed working on that movie, but my experience on 'Armour of God 3' felt more like the way he used to make movies with the action. However, afterward, I returned to Germany as I realized that I could not survive financially so easily.

RB: I know but what a fantastic experience and serving your apprenticeship under Jackie not to many people can put that on their CV.

AL: I really did not want to leave, but I had to return home to Germany to earn some proper money. However, I did receive the call back for 'Dragon Blade.' Working on this movie was also different, with a bigger crew, and Jackie did not have so much time for us on this shoot. But I always like how Jackie remembers me and how we met. This is special to me. He used to tell the other stunt guys when he was telling stories, 'You see this guy, well he hung around my film set for one week just to try to get noticed.' I would just look back at him and smile, and be grateful that my journey was now one of his stories (smiling)

RB: What a great story! Now, let's move forward and discuss how you landed the role in "Accident Man 2". As I have mentioned to some of the other cast members, this film provided a fantastic opportunity for everyone to showcase their talents, with each actor receiving excellent set pieces and screen time. This experience will undoubtedly enhance their resumes for future roles; I mean I really loved the movie.

AL: Yes, it was an excellent showcase, and I'm glad that you enjoyed the movie. I first

met Scott on the set of "Undisputed 4" when I was one of the fighters, and it was Tim Man, the fight choreographer, who got me involved. In the fight scene, I was paired up with Tim Man, and this was how I was introduced to Scott. During the fight, Scott accidentally injured me, and I had to receive a few stitches. Despite my desire to continue, the whole crew insisted that I rest and recover. I was impatient in the hospital and kept looking at my watch, worried that I would be replaced.

One thing about Scott is that he is very loyal to his team. Tim also provided some choreographed ideas for the Kirby brothers in "AM2." If Tim is not available, Scott usually reaches out to me to help with choreography. Initially, I was going to be the action director for the movie, but it turned out better to let George and Harry be in charge of the production since it was their first feature. The production being UK-based made it much more feasible. As a result, I only ended up doing my fight and Sarah's fight in the film.

RB: when I heard you only had two days to work out the fight scenes I said you must have been shooting two fights at the same time to keep it on scheduled.

AL: Yes, it is true. However, I initially believed that two days was sufficient time. I am accustomed to working with tighter deadlines than this due to the pace of work in Hong Kong. Nevertheless, I acknowledge that this timeline may be considered quite tight under Western rules and regulations.

RB: I have watched the movie twice - once at home before interviewing Scott, and then again at the London premiere with him. As a true Hong Kong movie fan, I must say that the fight scene between you and Scott was excellent and captured the essence of Hong Kong-style action. This kind of action is not often seen in Western-made movies as it is difficult to replicate without experience in that particular industry. During my interview with Scott, he also gave you a lot of credit for your involvement in the choreography. This fight scene

truly showcased your ability and was a highlight of the movie. The way it was shot was a great set piece and you could see the Jackie-style choreography flowing. And it was very well constructed, watching it a second time I am now locked in on the fight scenes and you and Scott pulled of a great ending even if you did look a bit like "Aaron Kwok" from "Saviour of the Soul" and it was like an end scene should be were you know the Villain and the hero are going to have a great fight scene.

AL: Thank you very much for your kind words. It's good to hear that from you. However, I can be very critical of my own work. For the scene, Scott invited me to play the main villain, where I get to kick his ass. I was careful in choosing something good to showcase, and during the fight scene, Scott and I put it together ourselves. I had a good idea of how it should look in the edit with the shot list, so we did some previews for the Kirby Brothers on the tripod. We placed it so we could get an idea of how the shots would look. Later, George came in and incorporated his camera movements into it. This was a very collaborative process that resulted in the final product. Despite this, I always think that I could have done better. However, I am my own worst critic.

RB: Also you can be up against time and budget and sometimes you just have to go with what you got in the can. But from a viewer's perspective watching it, they would have no complaints and the crowd loved it in the cinema the audience got to what we would say here in the in the UK some "Good Shapes". Like you see in the old Kung Fu movie flicks.

AL: Thank you, that's good to know. I sometimes wonder how they managed to produce so many high-quality movies even though they were shooting day and night. Sometimes, they would take a month to work on a single fight scene, yet they were still able to make six films in a year.
RB: so what you up to next when will we see you on the big screen again.

AL: Well, actually, I do not get to be seen in front of the camera when I work on a movie. I began my career as a stuntman and then moved on to action directing.

Although I would love to do more work in front of the camera, it hasn't been my primary focus.

RB: well we have talked for a long time and it was so great to hear your Jackie story and I really look forward to following your career an inviting you back to talk more about your future projects, Thank you so much Andy.

AL: no thank you it was great talking to you and I would love to come back and talk more as my career grows.

RB: thank you again Andy.

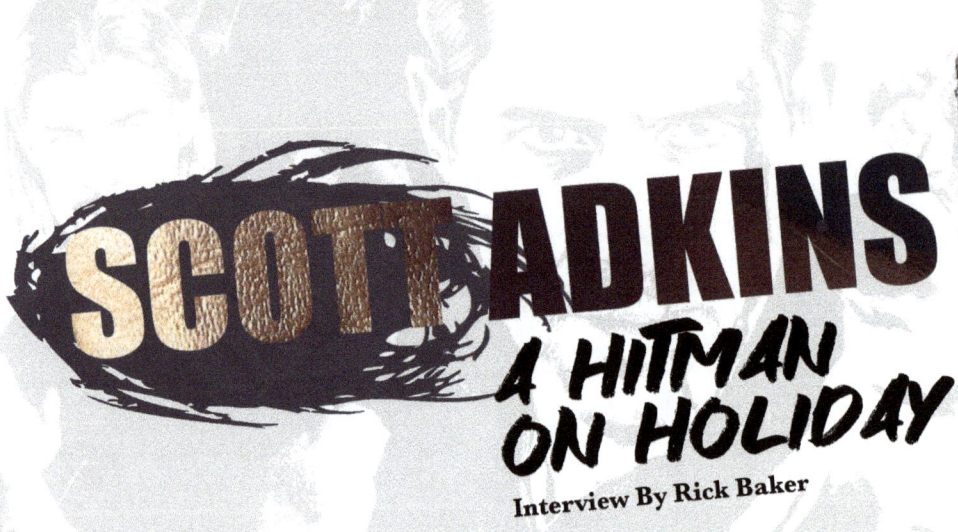

SCOTT ADKINS
A HITMAN ON HOLIDAY
Interview By Rick Baker

OVERVIEW.

Scott Adkins is a versatile actor known for his powerful performances in both major blockbuster hits and independent films. He has demonstrated a remarkable range in his career, showcasing his ability to embody complex and dramatic characters as well as thrill audiences with his exceptional martial arts skills.

Adkins' martial arts prowess sets him apart from other actors, allowing him to bring a level of realism and excitement to his action scenes. He is a highly skilled martial artist who has trained in various disciplines including Taekwondo, Kickboxing, Krav Maga, and Brazilian Jiu-Jitsu. His martial arts background has been a significant factor in landing him roles in action films such as "Undisputed" and "The Expendables 2," where he played opposite Hollywood legends Sylvester Stallone and Jean-Claude Van Damme.

Apart from his acting ability, Adkins is also a talented writer and producer. He has written and produced several of his own films showcasing his commitment to his craft and a desire to have a greater say in the films he is involved in.
Adkins' dedication and passion for his craft have not gone unnoticed in the industry, with his work being highly regarded by both critics and audiences. He has also been recognized with various awards and nominations for his performances, including the Best Supporting Actor Award at the 2020 Action on Film Festival for his role in "Ip Man 4: The Finale."
In summary, Scott Adkins is a highly talented actor who has made a name for himself in the industry with his exceptional martial arts skills, remarkable range as an actor, and dedication to his craft. His performances are a testament to his ability to bring authenticity and depth to each character he portrays, making him a standout in the industry.

IN THE BEGINNING.

I first met Scott in the early to mid-1990s, when my colleague Toby Russell and I decided to expand our regular screenings at London's Scala cinema and moved up North to "The Broadway Cinema" in Nottingham to put on double martial arts bills. This was where I first encountered Scott, and I believe I may have sold him a bootleg tape of "Tiger Cage 2". Through our cinema events, Scott got to know both me and my mother, who was always in attendance. His passion for "Hong Kong Style Action" was evident early on, as he was already creating homemade films, as many people did at the time, with often hilarious outcomes.

During this period, Toby and I were creating a video version of our magazine and thought it would be great to have a section featuring homemade Fu called "STOP KUNG FU". We began inviting people to submit their homemade movies, often shot in a living room, bedroom, or garden. When we mentioned this to Scott, he offered to contribute one of his own films to that section. When we watched it, we were pleasantly surprised to see Scott, looking like a handsome young version of Hugh Grant in a long dark coat, creating an action sequence with a few of his friends outdoors. This sequence highlighted the beginnings of a budding action movie star, with Scott's well-executed action and stances reminiscent of Chow Yun fat in "A Better Tomorrow".

We were so impressed with Scott's short film that we included it in one of the sections of our TV show, which was commissioned by the BBC with Jonathan Ross. We decided to call the section "STOP KUNG FU", and it featured one of Scott's short movies directed by "Ross Boysack" to showcase his on-screen abilities. By the time the show aired in 2001, Scott had already started his career in the industry, first with small TV roles and then appearing alongside Jackie Chan in "The Accidental Spy" (2001). From there, he went on to star in over 60 movies, becoming one of the biggest names in action movies. This is a remarkable achievement for anyone, and I am particularly proud to call him a friend who, like me, hails from the Midlands.

For a few years, I have wanted to pay tribute to Scott, and with the release of "Accident-man 2", it seemed like the perfect time to do so. I am thrilled to have the opportunity to talk to him about his latest movie, which was one of the best action films of 2022.

THE INTERVIEW

RB: It's great to see you, Scott. You're looking well, as always. Last night, I watched 'AM2', and I have to say that my partner enjoyed it a lot, which is quite impressive. I wanted to ask you whether it was always your intention to turn 'Accident Man' into a franchise and take Mike Fallon on various adventures when you were shooting the first movie?

SA: When I was just fourteen years old, around the same age I was visiting the "Broadway Cinema" in Nottingham, I received a comic book that I absolutely loved. It was incredibly violent and sadistic, with that unmistakable British 200-AD edge to it. At the time, I thought to myself secretly that it would make an incredible film. However, when I entered the film business in 2009/2010, I decided to inquire about the rights to the comic. Eventually, I was able to acquire them, and my friend Stu Small and I set out to write a script. We shopped it around, which took some time, but we eventually got it to Sony. As soon as they read the script, they were on board and ready to move forward with the film. At that point, I had never really considered the possibility of a sequel or franchise, but it certainly seemed like a potential possibility. Then we pitched the sequel, but there was a change in leadership at Sony, and coupled with the start of the pandemic, it took a while for the project to move forward.

RB: I know when writing a script often we look at where we can get the best tax breaks, your location was the sunny location of Valletta, Malta. Great location did this make the budget bigger for the sequel.

SA: I knew from the outset that we couldn't film the second movie in London, as the character had been banished from England in the first film. We also didn't want to shoot in Scotland or Wales. So, I knew that we wouldn't be filming in the UK, and if that meant going to another country like Thailand, then so be it.

Ultimately, we were able to shoot the film anywhere that gave us the necessary tax break, which would make it a more appealing location financially. That's how we ended up in Malta, which had a good tax break and also provided a stunning

backdrop for the movie. Filming in Malta gave the movie a completely different feel from the first one, which was really exciting.

RB: It really made a difference for me as it gave the film a more grandiose and expensive appearance. Right from the opening scene, where the drone zooms in on the first shot, it establishes the quality and tone of the movie.

SA: That's thanks to the guys who pushed to hire a drone operator, and the directors who wanted to achieve that particular look. They had already used a drone for filming in the UK, but if we had been shooting in the East End of London, it would have been much harder to get permission to fly a drone there. Luckily, in Malta, there were no problems. Even though the movie looks sun-drenched, we were actually filming during their heaviest rainy season. We encountered storms that managed to wash away some of our sets, and we even had to cancel one day due to the weather. Losing a day was a setback in the schedule, but we managed to make up for lost time when the sun came out.

RB: I noticed in your latest film, and I have been following your career since day one, that the camera angles and fight scenes are really on point. As you get older, do you find that your growing experience allows you to bring your A-game to movies that you produce and have greater control

RB: One of the things I liked about 'Accident Man 2' was how generous you were in giving all the actors a great showcase for their fight scenes, rather than having multiple fight scenes. It felt like a great addition to their CV when they go forward for another role. Often, some actors only have screen time of less than 30 seconds or are just one of the thugs. But in 'Accident Man 2,' everyone's fight scene stood out as its own set piece. Was that intentional?

SA: I have read a few reviews, and to be perfectly honest, it didn't occur to me at the time that I was being generous. When you think about some of the other action stars, they probably don't want any of the fighters to outshine them. But personally, I have never been like that. Take, for example, the "Undisputed" films. It's me and Isaac Florentine pushing for Marko Zaror and for "Ninja 2," Kane Kosugi, to make those fight scenes look as good and as impressive as possible. But at the end of the day, the script says I win and I am the hero, which is fair enough. But like Stallone, he always understood that you have to make your villains look good and that they are more than capable of kicking the shit out of you and then the hero. But at the end, the hero eventually wins, and I always think that the better they look and fight.

RB: I thought the film did justice for all the actors in the film particularly the fight scenes, I thought my old mate Beau Fowler came across well as "Poco" the clown, both his acting and his on screen fighting.

SA: Well, he did bring a lot to that character, and we had some issues with the original guy having COVID and having to isolate in his hotel room. So, Beau came in last minute, and he brought so much to that character, expanding beyond things that were not necessarily on the page. He was fantastic, a great actor, and he could also do all the fight scenes required of him. As a producer, that is what you're looking for.

RB: I mean another noteworthy character was the performance from "Sarah Chang" and I know I will not be the only one to say this, but when you two were on screen it reminded me of the same on screen

over keep pushing the bar in terms of acting and action?

SA: Yes, unfortunately, I have always been a late starter. But I'm now in a good place and trying to keep myself in shape because I feel that I've hit my stride as a filmmaker. I know what it takes, and when I look back at the first 'Accident Man,' I realize that it was on that film where I truly experienced what it was like to get creatively involved in both writing and producing. I also had a lot of influence over the way the film was executed, which became a turning point in my career. It was that moment when things began to improve and get better for me.

RB: So having more clout allowed you a better understanding of film making?

SA: Yes, it gave me a lot more confidence. In the early days, I thought I knew what I was doing, but in reality, I didn't. When I was on set, I would think to myself, 'Okay, the director knows what he's doing,' even though I would disagree with some of their decisions. I believed that they knew more than me because they were the director. But as time passed, I gained more confidence. With 'Accident Man,' we learned a lot, and the movie was successful. People liked it. So, you do get better, but at the same time, you have to prove it to yourself and take that leap.

relationship that "Peter Sellers" had with "Burt Kwok" in the "Pink panther movies.

SA: Well, I don't know if we paid homage, or we just 'ripped it off' (laughing), but I loved those movies from the 60s. There's a whole bunch of kids today that probably won't even know about those movies, so I figured we could get away with it. And I felt we could do it again, but with better action.

RB: Well, Sarah really shined, and I can see a big future for her. I mean, she played it well as a hard-nosed character rather than a sexy Asian babe, which films often cast for eye candy.

SA: Well, she really immersed herself and inhabited the character. She had good comic timing, did a lot of improvisation, and delivered with the action, so it worked well for the film. In fact, I am grateful to Mike Leeder because it was him who put me onto her.

RB: I thought the end fight scene between you and "Andy long" was an excellent end fight, which is what you want in a movie and the crowd certainly lapped it up at the screening we attended.

SA: Well the last two fights were by Andy and the end fight was an amalgamation was put together by a few people including the Kirby's and a little bit from "Tim man"

RB: was Tim on the set out there with you?

SA: No, he was not on set," "He had done some previews for some fights ages ago, back when the film was still in development. Eventually, the project got delayed and we ended up using only a few small elements from his previews. However, I still wanted to give him credit for his contributions, even though he was occupied with other work at the time and was unable to join us on the set. In fact, I actually did more choreography on this film than on any other movie I had previously worked on.

RB: Watching the film I felt that you had, had a much bigger hand in the fight scenes and it the action felt better to me.

SC: The good thing about this shoot was that George and Harry Kirby knew exactly where to position the camera, so there were no issues. We had great chemistry and agreed with each other on the action. Initially, I was on the lookout, ready to step in and say, 'That's not going to work. We need to do it this way,' because I've worked on many action films, and I've filmed and edited fight scenes myself in the past. However, I didn't have to intervene. Even during the previews we did back in London, we were in sync. They knew what to do, I knew what to do, and at times, George Kirby, one of the directors, was even holding the camera while we shot because he was a stuntman so he understands the action and how to shoot it.

RB: So can I ask you how much preparation do you put into a film like "AM2"?

SA: We spent two weeks shooting previews in London. Then, when the actors arrived in Malta, we had a week to rehearse before filming the final fight scene. Andy and I, mostly Andy, created that end fight together. It was a lot of work, but it ensured that on the day we were spending real money, we knew exactly what shots we needed to capture. We didn't want to leave anything on the cutting room floor, so we aimed to get the shots 'Hong Kong style.' This meant that we had a plan in place, and we executed it efficiently. We only had two days for each fight.

RB: Well, often than not in film

production, to create a good fight scene you do need time to get it nailed, but hearing the short time you had the fights looked great like you had spent weeks on them as they were some complicated set pieces.

SA: That's why you don't want to be making it up on the spot and figuring out what angles you need to use on the day. So, if you're prepared, you can go out and find some locations. Then, you can come back to London and map everything out in a gym with all the boxes set up so you know the space. This way, you can choreograph it as if you're on the location. However, the problem was that when we arrived, we lost two of the locations, which changed things. The opening fight scene with Sarah should have been much longer, but that wasn't our fault. It was due to production. Did you like the fact that Sarah character "Wong Sui-Ling's" was the descendant of "Wong Fei Hung"

RB: Yes, that was a nice little touch. I often look for Easter eggs when watching movies, but I liked that 'Nice Touch, mate.' I'll tell you what, I'll say it honestly: it's very hard for any other country to replicate Hong Kong's action comedy slapstick. It's one of Jackie's trademarks in most of his films, and it can be very difficult to duplicate. I think what you've brought to the screen here is fantastic. You've created a comedy with tons of action and British humour, which I really like. This is not an easy thing to replicate, and I doubt that there are many, if any, in the UK who could deliver at the same high level as you did in 'AM2.' It could make the movie an instant flop, I mean it's a very risky thing because if it is not done right its an automatic fail for the audiences.

SA: Well, that's great, and I'm glad to hear that from you, Rick. You know me, and we go way back. I was inspired by the movies you used to show at 'The Broadway Cinema.' I'll tell you what one of the big influences was for me, and it wasn't even a Hong Kong movie, but it's a Hong Kong movie in many ways. I loved those 'No Retreat, No Surrender' movies growing up that a Hong Kong Directors which in this case was "Corey Yuen". I found them so entertaining that I could find myself laughing but for all the wrong reasons. Still, it was brilliant entertainment, and I still love them to this day. It was my goal to make a movie that was as entertaining as that, but not laughing at us, but with us!

RB: In my opinion, for what it's worth, you have managed to strike the right balance, and I believe that you have reached a level in your film career where you can create good action sequences that seamlessly blend with comedy. However, if you have not had any experience working on a Hong Kong movie set or watched numerous Hong Kong Kung Fu movies, you may not realize how difficult it is to achieve this kind of balance.

SA: Comedy is a very challenging genre to tackle. For instance, in the "Shitting in the Bucket" scene in "AM2", some viewers may find it hilarious, while others may find it utterly repulsive. This type of humour might appeal more to UK audiences. Personally, I find this kind of comedy quite amusing, but it's something that you can only create for your own satisfaction.

RB: Yes some of the gags would be more appreciated by a British audience.

SA: You're absolutely correct. The comedy in "AM2" draws more influences from British humor than typical Hong Kong humour. To me, it reflects the kind of comedy that I enjoyed watching while growing up, such as the "Rik Mayall" toilet humour in shows like "Bottom" and "The Young Ones," as well as the style of humour in "Monty Python."

RB: However, I do believe that the American audience, who have access to many BBC programs through classic channels, have become more familiar with British comedy. In "AM2", there's a scene where you are working on your first job with Fred, and the background music sounds quite similar to the theme tune from "The Professionals"."

SA: I think they were aiming for it to be more "Mission Impossible" I mean as he was not an English composer I think he was probably 'riffling' more on "Mission Impossible".

RB: Looking at another character in the film, you did a great job of managing to portray "George Fouracre's" character, "Dante," as the most annoying person I have seen on screen for some time. I mean, you made me wish for his death from the first ten minutes of the movie, and I didn't mind when he was killed off at the end. (laughing).

SA: Well, that was the plan: to put "Accident Man," one of the best assassins in the world, with a kid so annoying that he desperately wants to kill him himself. He would love nothing more than to extinguish him on the spot, but he is forced to protect him, and that eats him up throughout the movie. However, I think George also made the character very funny, with a good balance of being annoying and amusing at the same time.

RB: I also enjoyed the scenes where "Fred" sets up all those devices to assassinate people, and how they were brought into the plot throughout the movie, especially the "Poco" scene. It was very well-done how you set them up to be used later in the film.

SA: That was something the directors brought to the table. We wanted those scenes to be in the Shambles, and I specifically requested both fights to be there because I knew that during the shoot, we would have to film both scenes simultaneously - one with me and "Poco," and one with Su Ling and Silas. This meant we had to dub the sound afterward because we were all shouting during filming. But that was the only way we could incorporate so much action with a shooting schedule of only 22 days. Then, George and Harry weaved the accidents into the "Poco" fight, which I loved. I was initially concerned that we might be stretching ourselves too thin with all the action we wanted and only 22 days to shoot, which was a real struggle. But it was a brilliant call from them, and after all, it is called "The Accident Man."

RB: well you did well, I thought before you mentioned that, that you had a 30 to 35 day shoot, but 22 days! That must have been full steam ahead no one sleeping to get it done (laughing).

SA: (laughing) My God, it would have been hard enough with a 30-day shoot back in the day. But that's why I'm producing it - so we can have two consecutive units. To be honest, I don't do these films for the enjoyment, because it's so stressful and physically demanding for me. I mean, come on, you don't get martial arts films like that anymore these days, do you Rick.

RB: Well, I was just about to say that you're jumping ahead to my next question. We've seen a declinc in Hong Kong martial arts movies in recent years, whether that's due to politics or censorship. To be honest, the last good martial arts film I saw was "Ip Man 4." A lot of people tag me in new movies that are coming out, and I don't want to be harsh, but frankly, they're just not that great or exciting. When I sat down to watch "AM2" with you, despite how well we know each other, if I didn't like it, I would have said so. But the film really flows well, and if you're into action, there are no real long pauses before we're into the next big set piece. I guess fans of this genre haven't seen this for a while. I mean, you can have a comedy film, and you can have an action film, but when you try to fuse the two together, it takes a very fine balance to make it work, as seen in the Jackie Chan films.

SA: Thanks, Rick. That's what you want to hear, as I love those movies, and I would like to try to keep that style going. I mean, I do a lot of films where the action is a bit more grounded, but I'm always trying to get more action in there. I love the Hong Kong-style action, so with "AM2," I thought we could go crazy with the fight scenes and deliver the fight action that I love watching.

RB: And that's what you see when watching "AM2." I don't know if it was more luck or just good judgment when casting the characters, as all the set pieces were excellent. But in particular, the fight between you and "Yendi," played by "Faisal Mohammed," who I had never seen before, was a great set piece.

SA: And that was a very technical fight scene to put together and he is a proper MMA fighter from the 90's fierce guy and we gave him a very technical set piece and remember he is a big guy wielded weapons at me.

RB: It was a really great looking scene, the way the pole was wielded about and the way the weapons were used it had a great look on the roof top.

SA: What you don't know is that as we were filming it started to rain, so we had to keep going back in and then when it stopped we would run back out and try to pick up the scene shouting "get the shot's Get the shot's" (laughing) so in the edit you will see it cutting to different shots but honestly the rain screwed us.

RB: Well, I will stand by my first comment. It looked like it could have been a period scene, and it was a long scene. So however, the rain affected you, it certainly did not show on the final cut. But that was like every fight scene you had in the film - it was a great showcase not only for you but also for the person you were fighting.

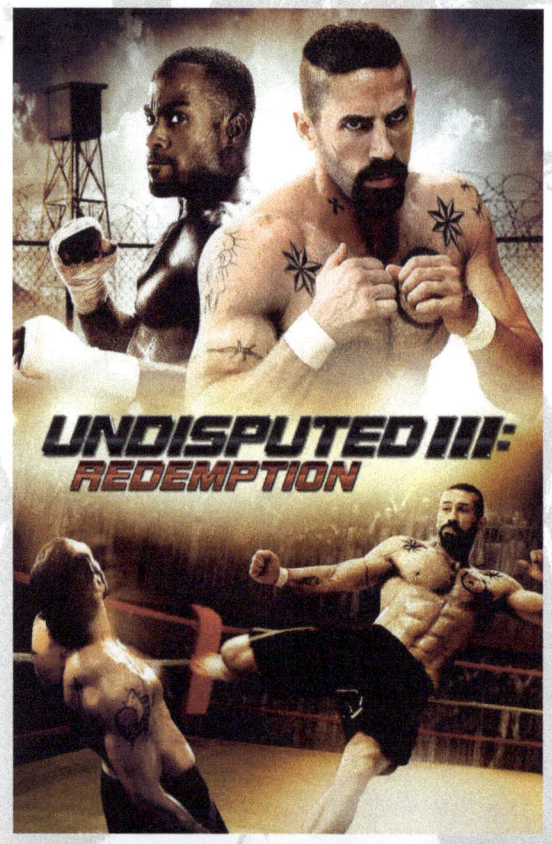

RB: good tip, can I ask how did you get Peter lee on board who also looked good in his scene?

SA: Well, he is a friend of Marko Zaror, and he has a great look similar to Brad Pitt. He is a good martial artist, both as a boxer and kickboxer, and I thought he seemed like a good fit for the character. So we said, let's get him in. He's a nice guy who works hard.

RB: Are you very much involved in the casting?

SA: Absolutely! That's why I'm producing it! And I'm very particular with who I bring into the film, especially if I have to fight them. You don't want to be messing around with someone who is no good, because that just makes my life so much harder. And when you have only two days to put the fight scene together, you need to be working with someone who flows with you and picks up things quickly. I know who is out there that can screen fight and act.

RB: Ok and finally let's talk about "Perry Benson", who plays Frank, I felt he was a great asset to the movie I mean he was in the first one and he certainly is a funny guy?

SC: Well, it was continuing the 'bromance' theme of "Friends and Family." Even if you're a stone-cold killer, you still need mates you can rely on, and that was our little thing. It was like an Edgar Rice themed movie.

RB: And he is a familiar face from British TV, who I have seen many times and he captures that sort of cuddly guy who you would want to protect and I liked the happy ending you gave to him that his so called scamming date was actually true even though it did not work.

SA: That was probably the only thing I was disappointed about - the final scene. We were in that pub a lot during filming, including the big scene with Ray, and we had so many characters. Unfortunately, we had to rush that scene and work to a short schedule. We weren't afforded the luxury to go back and reshoot a scene, so it was a case of what we got is what we got! Sadly, that scene just wasn't working because we were being too ambitious on that day. In the movie, you see it ends quite abruptly, unfortunately. But hey, that's my excuse, and that was one of the things that I personally was disappointed about. And there was more to it.

RB: I thought that after it ended, with Su Ling saying that she was going to hunt her down and find her, and to be honest, I thought you might have been setting up another plot for part three. But, to be honest with you, and this is just my personal thought, "AM2" was one of the best action films of 2022. The reason is I loved the British-style humour, but it was so heart-warming to see this kind of Hong Kong-style comedy, along with great fighting.

SA: (Laughing) And I am calling people 'Stupid Burke' and 'absolute Twat.' I mean, you can't get much more British than that when you add that to your dialogue.

RB: It was a bit 'Black Adder' style to me, and it resonated with my humour. Whether that is everyone's cup of tea, I doubt it, but it certainly tickled me, almost in a 'Carry on film' mode. We are both from the Midlands, and we both share that sense of humour more than others.

SA: I think for me you should make films for yourself, if you start to predict what other people want then it can be difficult, I mean maybe you should but with "AM2" I making films for myself what I like.

RB: Well, Scott, thank you for taking the time to speak with me. I hope you'll enjoy reading this magazine when it comes out. I think it shows how much I loved the film, wanting to dedicate a complete issue to it. And I know that 2023 is going to be another great year for you. I, for one, will be looking forward to your next project and hopefully sitting back down with you to discuss that. So, best of luck with all your new projects.

SA: thanks Rick mate was good talking to you mate and yes let us catch up again.

SA: Well, one thing I tell the actors is that they have to bring charm to their character. We can all stand there and look mean, but when you throw a well-executed kick, you don't have to keep looking mean. Just do anything else but look mean.